THE PSALMS
IN
INCLUSIVE
LANGUAGE

JOSEPH J. ARACKAL, V.C.

Translator

A Liturgical Press Book

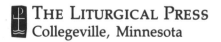

THE LITURGICAL PRESS
Collegeville, Minnesota

Cover design by Mary Jo Pauly.

1	2	3	4	5	6	7	8

Library of Congress Cataloging-in-Publication Data

Bible. O.T. Psalms. English. Arackal. 1993.
    Psalms in inclusive language / Joseph J. Arackal.
       p.   cm.
    ISBN 0-8146-2024-8
    I. Arackal, Joseph J., 1942–   . II. Title.
BS1424.A73   1993
223'.205209—dc20   92-32647
                                                CIP

To the members of the Vincentian Congregation

A memento of the 25th Anniversary of my Ordination
1967 – December 16 – 1992

Contents

Contents

Contents

Preface

Psalms are prayers expressive of deep human feelings that manifest cries of praise, entreaty or thanksgiving. In some of the Psalms, however, the psalmists imprecate enemies for their malicious and unjust behavior. So the language used in the psalms naturally evokes those profound sentiments.

The Psalms in Inclusive Language is the product of my conviction that inclusive language is essential in nourishing, strengthening and expressing Faith. The use of inclusive language in worship and in scripture translations is matter of justice and the continued use of exclusive language a serious injustice.

Inclusive language is understood as a way of expressing one's concern for using words that do not exclude, or express prejudice against individuals or groups regardless of gender, attributes such as color, race, culture, nationality, lifestyle or physical characteristics. Inclusive language recognizes the inherent value of all human beings and does not limit their understanding of God. Inclusive language is much wider in its scope than gender-fair language but obviously includes it.

Language, especially in the context of religion, is a very powerful tool in the formation of cultural and social attitudes. While inclusive language can truly enhance, augment, sustain, inspire and express faith, exclusive language can have lasting negative results.

The Study of scriptures, both the Old Testament and the New Testament, reveals that the original scripture texts were inclusive in nature, but their translations into some of the modern languages have resulted in much of the exclusive language and expressions in the present scripture translations.

My sincere thanks to all those who by their encouragement and constant support assisted me in the preparation of *The Psalms in Inclusive Language*. Special thanks are due to Rev. Thomas Wahl, O.S.B, St. John's University, Collegeville, Minnesota, for his extensive reviews, comments and suggestions and to Eileen E. Effertz, Belle Plaine, Minnesota, for her assistance in the preparation and proofreading of the manuscript.

BOOK ONE
Psalms 1-41

PSALM 1
The Two Ways

1 Blessed are they
who reject the counsel of the wicked,
follow not the way of sinners,
and sit not in the company of perjurers.
2 Their delight is in the law of Yahweh,
and they meditate on it day and night.

3 They are like a tree planted near streams,
which yields its fruit in its season,
and whose leaves never wither.
They prosper in all that they do.

4 Not so are the wicked;
but they are like chaff
which the wind drives about.
5 The wicked will not do well in the judgment,
nor sinners in the assembly of the just.

6 For Yahweh knows the way of the just,
but the way of the wicked will perish.

PSALM 2
The Universal Reign of the Messiah

1 Why do the nations conspire,
and the peoples plot in vain?
2 The rulers of the earth rise up,
and the sovereigns plot together
against Yahweh and the anointed one:
3 "Let us break their bonds,
and let us throw off their cords from us."

4   The One Who sits in the heavens laughs;
    Adonai shall mock at them.
5   Then God will speak to them in anger,
    and will terrify them in wrath:
6   "I have set My ruler on Zion,
    My holy mount."

7   I will proclaim the decree of Yahweh:
    God said to me: "You are My child,
    today I have begotten you.
8   Ask of Me, and I will give you
    the nations as your inheritance,
    and the utmost parts of the earth
    as your possession.
9   You shall break them with a rod of iron,
    and smash them like an earthen vessel."

10 Now then, O rulers, be wise;
    O judges of the earth, be warned.
11 Serve Yahweh with reverence,
    and rejoice with trembling.
12 Pay homage, lest Yahweh be angry,
    and you perish from your way;
    for God's anger is quickly kindled.
    Blessed are they who seek refuge in Yahweh.

PSALM 3
A Prayer for Deliverance

A Psalm of David, when he fled from his son Absalom.

1   O Yahweh, how countless are my adversaries!
    How many are there who rise against me?
2   Many are saying of me,
    'there is no help for you in God.'

3   But You, O Yahweh, are a shield around me,
    my glory, You hold my head high.

4 I cry aloud to You, Yahweh,
    You hear me from Your holy mountain.

5 I lie down and sleep;
    I wake again, for You, Yahweh, sustain me.

6 I am not afraid of the thousands of people
    who have set themselves against me all around.

7 Arise, O Yahweh! Deliver me, O my God!
    For You have struck all my foes on the jaw;
    You have broken the teeth of the wicked.

8 Deliverance belongs to You, Yahweh;
    Your blessing be upon Your people!

PSALM 4
A Night Prayer of Confidence

To the choir director: with stringed instruments.
A Psalm of David.

1 When I call, answer me, O God of my justice!
    You comforted me when I was in distress.
    Have mercy on me, and hear my prayer.

2 O people, how long shall my honor suffer shame?
    How long will you love vanity, chase after lies?

3 But know that Yahweh has set apart the devout;
    Yahweh hears when I call.

4 Tremble and do not sin;
    commune with your own heart
    and on your bed meditate and be still.

5 Offer the sacrifices of justice,
    and put your trust in Yahweh.

6 There are many who say,
    "O that we might see some good!"
    Lift up the light of Your face on us!

7 O Yahweh, You have put more joy in my heart,
    than they have when their grain and wine abound.

8   In peace I will both lie down and sleep,
     for You alone, O Yahweh, make me dwell in safety.

PSALM 5
A Morning Prayer for Guidance

To the choir director: with flutes.
A Psalm of David.

1   Give ear to my words, O Yahweh;
     and give heed to my petitions.

2   Attend to the sound of my cry,
     Adonai and my God,
     for to You do I pray.

3   O Yahweh, at daybreak You hear my voice;
     at daybreak I set myself before You,
     and fix my eyes on You.

4   For You are not a God Who delights in wickedness;
     nor shall evil live in Your presence.

5   The boastful shall not stand before Your eyes;
     You detest all workers of iniquity.

6   You, O Yahweh, destroy those who speak lies;
     You despise the bloodthirsty and the deceitful.

7   But I will come into Your house,
     in the abundance of Your faithful love,
     I will worship in Your holy temple with reverence.

8   Lead me in Your saving justice, O Yahweh,
     on account of my enemies;
     make Your way straight before me.

9   For there is no truth in their mouths;
     in their hearts is wickedness;
     their throat is an open grave;
     they flatter with their tongues.

10 Make them bear their guilt, O God;
     let them fall by their own counsels;

drive them away because of their revolt,
for they have rebelled against You.

11 But let all who trust in You rejoice,
let them ever sing for joy,
because You defend them;
let those who love Your Name be joyful in You.
12 For You bless the just, O Yahweh;
You cover them with favor as with a shield.

PSALM 6
A Prayer of Faith for Healing:
First Penitential Psalm

To the choir director: with stringed instruments;
on an eight-stringed harp. A Psalm of David.

1 O Yahweh, reprove me not in Your anger,
nor chastise me in Your wrath.
2 Have mercy on me, O Yahweh, for I am languishing;
O Yahweh, heal me, for my bones are troubled.
3 My soul also is greatly troubled.
But You, O Yahweh, how long. . .?

4 Return, O Yahweh, save my soul;
save me because of Your faithful love.
5 For in death there is no remembrance of You;
and who shall worship You in Sheol?

6 I am weary with my groaning;
every night I flood my bed chamber with weeping;
I soak my bed with my tears.
7 My eyes are dim because of grief,
they grow weak because of all my enemies.

8 Depart from me, all you who work iniquity;
for Yahweh has heard the sound of my weeping.
9 Yahweh has heard my supplication;
Yahweh will accept my prayer.

10   Let all my enemies be ashamed
     and greatly troubled;
     they shall turn back, ashamed in a moment.

PSALM 7
A Prayer for Deliverance from Enemies

A Shiggaion—A Lament of David, which he sang to Yahweh
concerning Cush a Benjaminite.

1   O Yahweh my God, in You do I take refuge;
    save me from all my pursuers, and deliver me.
2   Let them not tear me apart like a lion,
    shredding me to pieces, with no one to rescue me.

3   O Yahweh my God, if I have done this,
    if iniquity has stained my hands,
4   if I have repaid my friend with evil
    or plundered my enemy without cause,
5   let the enemy pursue me and overtake me,
    and let them trample my life to the ground,
    and lay my honor in the dust.

6   Arise, O Yahweh, in Your anger;
    lift Yourself up against the fury of my enemies;
    awake, O my God, to the judgment You have
      appointed.
7   Let the assembly of the peoples be gathered about You;
    and over it take Your seat on high;
    for You, Yahweh, will judge the peoples.

8   Judge me, O Yahweh, according to my justice
    and according to the integrity that is in me.
9   O let the malice of the wicked come to an end,
    but sustain the just,
    You just God, Who discern minds and hearts.

10   My defense is God,
     Who saves the upright of heart.

11 God is a just judge,
   is angry with the wicked every day.

12 If they do not repent,
   God will sharpen the sword,
   bend the bow and make it ready.
13 God has prepared the instruments of death
   and will make arrows hot for pursuers.

14 Behold, the wicked conceive malice,
   are pregnant with iniquity,
   and give birth to deception.
15 They make a pit, digging it out,
   but fall into the hole which they have made.
16 Their mischief returns on their own heads,
   and on their own crowns their violence descends.

17 I will give to You, Yahweh,
   the thanks due to Your justice,
18 and I will sing praise to the name of Yahweh,
   the Most High.

PSALM 8
A Hymn Celebrating God's Infinite Majesty

To the choir director: on an instrument of Gath.
A Psalm of David.

1 O Yahweh, our God,
   how majestic is Your Name in all the earth!

   You have exalted Your majesty above the heavens.
2 Out of the mouth of babes and infants,
   You have fashioned praise because of Your enemies,
   to still the enemy and the revenger.

3 When I look at Your heavens,
   the work of Your fingers,
   the moon and the stars which You have set in place;

19

4   who are the humans that You are mindful of them,
    and the human beings that You visit them?

5   Yet You have made them little less than a god,
    and crowned them with glory and honor.
6   You have given them dominion
    over the works of Your hands;
    You have put all things under their feet:

7   all sheep and oxen,
    and also the beasts of the country,
8   the birds of the air,
    and the fish of the sea,
    and all that swim the paths of the sea.

9   O Yahweh, our God,
    how majestic is Your Name in all the earth!

PSALM 9
A Prayer of Thanksgiving for God's Justice

To the choir director: to the tune of "Muth-labben."
A Psalm of David.

1   I will give thanks to Yahweh with my whole heart;
    I will tell of all Your wonderful deeds.
2   I will rejoice and delight in You,
    I will sing praise to Your Name, O Most High.

3   When my enemies turned back,
    they stumbled and perished before You.
4   For You have maintained my just cause;
    You have sat on the throne giving just judgment.

5   You have rebuked the nations,
    You have destroyed the wicked;
    You have put out their name for ever and ever.
6   The enemy have vanished in everlasting ruins;
    their cities have been rooted out;
    the very memory of them has perished.

7   But You, Yahweh, sit enthroned for ever,
    You have established Your throne for judgment;
8   and You judge the world with justice,
    You judge the peoples with equity.
9   Yahweh, You are the Savior of the oppressed,
    a refuge in times of trouble.
10 And those who know Your Name
    put their trust in You, O Yahweh,
    You do not forsake those that seek You.

11 Sing praises to Yahweh, the Ruler of Zion;
    announce Yahweh's deeds among the peoples.
12 For You remember the laments of those who mourn,
    You do not forget the cry of the afflicted.

13 Have mercy on me, O Yahweh!
    Behold what I suffer from those who hate me,
    O You Who pull me back from the gates of death,
14 that I may recount all Your praises,
    at the gates of the city of Zion
    and rejoice in Your deliverance.

15 The nations have sunk in the pit which they made;
    their feet are caught in the net they hid.
16 Yahweh has been made known, and has executed
        judgment;
    the wicked are snared in the work of their own hands.

17 The wicked shall be turned back to Sheol,
    and all the nations that forget God.
18 For the needy shall not for ever be forgotten,
    and the hope of the poor shall not perish for ever.

19 Arise, O Yahweh!
    let human strength not prevail;
    the nations shall stand trial before You!
20 O Yahweh, strike them with terror!
    Let the nations know that they are but humans!

PSALM 10
Prayer for Divine Intervention Against
the Wicked

1   Why do You stand afar off, O Yahweh?
    Why do You hide Yourself in times of trouble?
2   In arrogance the wicked pursue the poor;
    they will be caught in the schemes
    which they have devised.

3   For the wicked boast of the desires of their hearts,
    and the greedy curse and renounce Yahweh.
4   The wicked in their arrogance do not seek God;
    all their thoughts are, "There is no God."

5   Their ways are perverted at all times;
    Your judgments are far from their minds;
    as for their rivals, they scoff at them all.
6   They all think in their hearts,
    "I shall not be moved;
    I shall never meet adversity."

7   Their mouth is full of cursing, deceit and oppression;
    under their tongue are mischief and iniquity.
8   They sit in the hiding-places of the villages;
    in the secret places they murder the innocent,
    their eyes spy upon the unfortunate.

9   They lie in wait secretly like a lion in its den;
    they lie in ambush that they may seize the poor,
    they seize the poor drawing them into their net.

10 The feeble, being crushed, bow down,
    and fall by the might of the powerful.
11 The wicked think in their hearts,
    "God has forgotten, and has turned away;
    God will never see it."

12 Arise, O Yahweh my God, raise Your hand;
    do not forget the poor.

13 Why should the wicked despise God,
and say in their hearts,
"You will not call us to account"?

14 Yes, You do see;
You do notice the misery of the poor,
that You may take them into Your hands;
the unfortunate commit themselves to You;
You have been the helper of the orphan.

15 You break the power of the wicked and the evil;
You punish their wickedness until You find none.
16 Yahweh reigns for ever and ever;
the wicked shall perish from the earth.

17 O Yahweh, You hear the laments of the poor;
You strengthen their will,
You listen to their cry:
18 to do justice to the orphans and the oppressed,
so that the worldly may strike terror no more.

PSALM 11
A Song of Trust in Yahweh, the Just One

To the choir director. Of David.

1 In Yahweh I take refuge;
how can you say to me,
"Flee to the mountains like a bird!

2 For behold! the wicked string their bows,
they make their arrow ready on the string,
to shoot the just in the darkness of night.
3 If the foundations are destroyed,
what can the just do"?

4 You, O Yahweh, are in Your holy temple,
You, O Yahweh, are enthroned in heaven;
Your eyes, O Yahweh, behold,
and Your glances scrutinize all humanity.

5 You, O Yahweh, scrutinize the just and the wicked,
  and You detest those that love violence.
6 You rain down calamities on the wicked;
  fire, brimstone and a scorching wind shall be their lot.

7 For You, O Yahweh, are just,
  You love just deeds;
  the just shall behold Your face.

PSALM 12
A Prayer for Deliverance from
Personal Enemies

To the choir director: for eight-stringed instruments.
A Psalm of David.

1 Help, Yahweh; for the good has ceased;
  the faithful have disappeared from the human race.
2 Everyone utter lies to their neighbors;
  they speak with flattering lips and a double mind.

3 Yahweh shall destroy those with flattering lips,
  and with tongues that speak proud things.
4 They say: "We shall prevail with our tongues,
  our lips are our own; who rules over us?"

5 "For the poor who are despoiled,
  for the needy who groan,
  I will now arise," says Yahweh;
  "I will grant safety to those who long for it."

6 The words of Yahweh are pure words,
  like silver refined in an earthen furnace,
  purified seven times.

7 You, O Yahweh, shall protect them,
  You shall preserve them from this crowd for ever.
8 On every side the wicked walk around,
  as corruption is exalted by all humanity.

PSALM 13
A Confident Prayer in Time of Sorrow

To the choir director. A Psalm of David.

1 How long, O Yahweh?
Will You forget me for ever?
How long will You hide Your face from me?
2 How long must I bear pain in my soul,
sorrow in my heart day and night?
How long shall my enemy be exalted over me?

3 Look down and answer me, O Yahweh, my God;
Give light to my eyes,
lest I fall into the sleep of death;
4 lest my enemy say, "I have prevailed over You";
lest my enemies rejoice because I am shaken.

5 But I have trusted in Your faithful love;
my heart shall rejoice in Your saving help.
6 I will sing to You Yahweh,
because You have dealt bountifully with me.

PSALM 14
A Lament over Widespread Corruption

To the choir director. Of David.

1 The fools say in their hearts, "There is no God."
They are corrupt, they do abominable deeds,
there are none that do good.

2 Yahweh looks down from heaven upon the human race,
to see if there be one who ponders,
one who searches for God.

3 They have all gone astray,
they are all alike corrupt;
there is none who does good,
no, not one.

4   Will all these evildoers never learn,
    they who devour my people as they eat bread?
    They have not called on Yahweh.

5   There they shall be in great fear,
    for God is with the just generation.
6   The wicked frustrate the plans of the poor,
    but Yahweh is their refuge.

7   O that deliverance for Israel would come out of Zion!
    When Yahweh restores the well-being of the people,
    Jacob shall rejoice, Israel shall be glad.

PSALM 15
The Guest of Yahweh

A Psalm of David.

1   O Yahweh, who shall dwell in Your tent?
    Who shall live on Your holy mountain?

2   Whoever lives with integrity,
    who practices justice,
    who speaks the truth from the heart;

3   who does not deceive with the tongue,
    who causes no evil to a friend,
    and accepts no bribe against a neighbor;

4   who detests the disobedient,
    but honors those who revere Yahweh,
    and stands by an oath at any cost;

5   who does not lend money at usury,
    and accepts no bribe against the innocent.
    Whoever does these shall never be removed.

PSALM 16
A Profession of Faith

A Miktam of David.

1 Watch over me, O God,
for I put my trust in You.
2 I say to Yahweh, "You are my God;
I have no goodness except in You."

3 As for the holy ones who are on the earth,
they are the glorious,
and in them is all my delight.
4 Those who run after other gods
shall multiply their sorrows;
I will not offer blood libations to them,
nor will I take their names upon my lips.

5 Yahweh is my allotted destiny
and my cup of blessing;
You shall surely uphold my destiny.
6 The measuring lines have fallen in agreeable sites;
yes, I have a beautiful inheritance.

7 I bless Yahweh who gives me counsel;
and even in the night instructs my mind.
8 I set Yahweh always before me;
with Yahweh at my right hand,
I shall not be removed.

9 Therefore my heart is glad,
my soul rejoices,
and my body also rests with confidence.
10 For You will not leave my soul in Sheol,
You will not allow Your holy one to see corruption.

11 You will make known to me the way of life;
in Your presence there is fullness of joy,
at Your right side there is happiness for ever.

PSALM 17
A Prayer of Confidence of
an Innocent Person

A Prayer of David.

1 O Yahweh, hear my just cause,
    listen to my cry!
    Give ear to my prayer from lips without deceit!
2 Let my vindication come from Your presence!
    Let Your eyes see what is right!

3 If You search my heart,
    if You visit me in the night,
    if You try me by fire,
    You shall find no wickedness in me;
    I have not sinned with my mouth.

4 With regard to the works of people,
    by the word of Your lips,
    I am kept from the paths of the violent.
5 My steps have been kept in Your tracks,
    that my feet may not stumble.

6 I call upon You, God, for You answer me,
    incline Your ear to me, hear my words.
7 Show Your marvelous faithful love,
    O Savior of those who trust in You.
    By Your right hand save me
    from those who rise up against You.

8 Guard me as the pupil, the apple of Your eye,
    hide me in the shadow of Your wings,
9 from the anger of the wicked who oppress me,
    and from my enemies who surround me.

10 Engrossed in themselves,
    their mouths speak arrogantly.
11 They are advancing against me, they surround me;
    looking for the chance to throw me to the ground.

12   They are like a lion hungry to devour,
      like young lions lurking in their hidden dens.

13   Arise, O Yahweh! confront them, overthrow them!
      Deliver my life from the wicked by Your sword,
14   with Your hand from the powerful ones, O Yahweh,
      from the worldly whose portion in life is of the world.

      You fill their avaricious bellies with treasures;
      they have enough riches for their children,
      and they bequeath their riches to their little ones.

15   As for me, I shall look upon Your face in truthfulness;
      when I awake, I shall be satisfied with Your presence.

PSALM 18
A Royal Song of Thanksgiving

To the choir director.
A Psalm of David the servant of Yahweh,
who sang to Yahweh the words of this song,
when Yahweh delivered him from the hands of
all his enemies, and from the hand of Saul.

1   I love You, O Yahweh, my strength.
2   Yahweh is my stronghold,
     my fortress, and my deliverer.
     My God, my Rock, in You I seek refuge.
     You are my shield,
     my saving strength, and my stronghold.

3   I call upon Yahweh, Who is worthy of praise,
     and I am saved from my enemies.

4   The cords of death hemmed me in,
     the surge of the ungodly overwhelmed me.
5   The cords of Sheol entangled me,
     the snares of death confronted me.

6   In my distress I called on Yahweh;
    and I cried for help to You my God.
    From Your temple You heard my voice,
    and my cry to You reached Your ears.

7   Then the earth shook and trembled;
    the foundations of the mountains moved
    and were shaken because of Your blazing anger.
8   Smoke went up from Your nostrils,
    and devouring fire from Your mouth;
    and coals were kindled by it.

9   You bowed the heavens, and came down;
    thick darkness was under Your feet.
10 You rode on a cherub, and flew;
    You came swiftly upon the wings of the wind.

11 You made darkness Your covering around You,
    dark, misty rain-clouds Your wrap.
12 Out of the brightness of Your shadow
    Your clouds rained hailstones and flashes of fire.

13 You, O Yahweh, also thundered in the heavens,
    and You, O Most High, uttered Your voice -
    hailstones and flashes of fire.
14 You shot Your arrows, and scattered them;
    You flashed forth lightning, and routed them.

15 Then the very springs of the ocean were exposed,
    and the foundations of the world were laid bare,
    at Your rebuke, O Yahweh,
    at the blast of the breath of Your nostrils.

16 You reached down from on high, snatched me up,
    You drew me out of watery depths.
17 You delivered me from my strong enemy,
    and from those who hated me;
    for they were too powerful for me.

18 They came upon me in the day of my calamity;
    but You, Yahweh, came to my support.
19 You brought me forth into freedom;
    You delivered me, because You love me.

20 Yahweh, You rewarded me because I was just,
    because my hands were innocent You repaid me.
21 For I have kept the ways of Yahweh,
    and have not revolted against my God.

22 For all Your ordinances are before me,
    and Your laws I have never put away from me.
23 I have always been virtuous before You,
    and I have carefully kept myself away from sins.

24 And You, Yahweh, repaid me because I was just,
    because my hands were innocent in Your sight.
25 With the faithful You show Yourself faithful;
    With the perfect You show Yourself perfect;

26 You show Yourself as pure with the pure;
    You appear villainous with the crooked.
27 For You save those who are humble,
    but humiliate those with haughty looks.

28 Yahweh, You Yourself are my lamp,
    You, Yahweh my God, enlighten my darkness.
29 With You I have pursued a band of robbers;
    and with You my God, I have leaped over a wall.

30 As for You, O God, Your way is perfect;
    Your word, Yahweh, is pure;
    You are a shield to all who trust in You.

31 For there is no God, besides Yahweh;
    and there is no one mighty like our God.
32 You, my God, gird me with strength,
    and make my way perfect.

33 You make me swift as a deer,
    and set me firmly upon high places.
34 You train my hands for battle,
    and strengthen my arms like a bow of brass.

35 You have given me the shield of safety,
    Your right hand has sustained me,
    and Your discipline has made me great.
36 You have steadied my legs under me,
    that my ankles may not be weakened.

37 I have pursued my enemies and overtaken them;
    and did not turn back till they were destroyed.
38 I have shattered them that they cannot rise;
    they fell under my feet.

39 You girded me with strength for battle;
    You subdued under me those who rose up against me.
40 You also defeated my enemies before me,
    that I might silence those who hate me.

41 They cried but there was none to save them,
    to You Yahweh, but You did not answer them.
42 I crumbled them like dust before the wind,
    trampled them like the mud of the streets.

43 You delivered me from the venom of the people;
    You made me the head of the nations;
    a people I have not known, now serve me.

44 As soon as they heard of me they obeyed me;
    foreign nations submitted themselves to me.
45 Foreign nations grew faint of heart,
    and came trembling out of their fortresses.

46 Yahweh lives;
    blessed be the One Who gave me strength,
    may God my Savior be exalted.
47 It is God Who avenged me,
    and subdued peoples under me.

48 You delivered me from my raging enemies;
    You lifted me high above those who attacked me;
    You delivered me from those who love violence.
49 For this I give thanks to You,
    O Yahweh, among the nations,
    and sing praises to Your Name.

50 You gave victories to Your ruler
    and showed kindness to Your anointed,
    to David and his posterity for ever.

PSALM 19
Hymn to Yahweh, the Creator and Lawgiver

To the choir director. A Psalm of David.

1 The heavens proclaim Your glory, O God,
   the firmament manifests Your handiwork.
2 Day unto day pours forth speech,
   and night unto night reveals knowledge.

3 There is no speech, nor are there words,
   where their voice is not heard.
4 Their voice goes out through all the earth,
   and their words to the end of the world.

   High above, You pitched a tent for the sun,
5 and it comes forth from its pavilion like a groom,
   like a champion who runs the course with joy.

6 At one end of the heavens it comes forth,
   and its course is to the other end;
   and nothing can escape its heat.

7 The law of Yahweh is perfect,
      refreshing the soul;
   the decree of Yahweh is trustworthy,
      making the simple wise;

8   the precepts of Yahweh are right,
         rejoicing the heart;
     the commandment of Yahweh is clear,
         enlightening the eyes;

9   the reverence of Yahweh is pure,
         enduring for ever;
     the ordinances of Yahweh are true,
         and all of them perfectly just.

10   They are more precious than gold,
         than precious stones;
     sweeter also than honey
         and drops from the honeycomb.

11   Your servant is formed by them;
         in keeping them there is great reward.
12   Can one ever discern all one's errors?
     Acquit me from my hidden faults.

13   Preserve Your servant from sins of pride,
     do not let them rule over me!
     Then I shall be innocent,
     and shall be free of serious sin.

14   Let the words of my mouth
     and the meditation of my heart
     be acceptable in Your sight,
     O Yahweh, my helper and my Savior.

PSALM 20
Prayer for the Ruler in Time of War

To the choir director. A Psalm of David.

1   May Yahweh answer you in the day of trouble!
     May the name of the God of Jacob protect you!
2   May Yahweh send you help from the sanctuary,
     and strengthen you out of Zion!

3 May God remember all your offerings,
  and make acceptable your burnt sacrifices!
4 May God grant you your heart's desire,
  and fulfill all your plans!

5 We will shout for joy over your victory,
  we will set up banners in the name of our God.
  May Yahweh grant all your petitions!

6 Now I know that Yahweh will help the anointed;
  God will answer from the holy heaven
  with the saving strength of God's right hand.

7 Some trust in chariots, and some in horses;
  but we call on the name of Yahweh our God.
8 They have bowed down and have fallen;
  but we have risen and stand ready.

9 Save! O Yahweh, our Ruler,
  answer us when we call.

PSALM 21
A Psalm of Thanksgiving for the Victory

To the choir director. A Psalm of David.

1 Yahweh, I rejoice in Your power,
  and greatly rejoice in Your saving help!
2 You have given me my heart's desire,
  and have not denied the prayer of my lips.

3 For You have blessed me with blessings of goodness;
  and You have set a precious crown on my head.
4 I asked life of You; You gave it to me,
  even length of days for ever and ever.

5 My glory is great through Your help;
  You have bestowed upon me honor and majesty.
6 You made me most blessed for ever;
  You made me glad with the joy of Your presence.

7 For I trust in Yahweh and shall remain unshaken,
   and trust in the faithful love of the Most High.
8 Your hand will reach all Your enemies;
   Your right hand will reach those who hate You.

9 You will set them as a blazing oven
   on the day of Your appearance.
   Yahweh will swallow them up in anger;
   and fire will consume them.

10 You will purge the earth of their offspring,
    the human race of their descendants.
11 If they plan evil against You,
    if they devise mischief, they will not succeed.

12 For You will put them to flight;
    You will aim at their faces with Your bow.
13 Be exalted, O Yahweh, in Your strength!
    We will sing and praise Your power.

PSALM 22
A Prayer of the Just in Time of Distress

To the choir director: to the tune of "The Deer of the Dawn."
A Psalm of David.

1 My God, my God, why have You forsaken me?
   Why are You so far from my deliverance,
   and from the words of my cry in distress?
2 O my God, I cry by day, but You do not answer;
   and by night, but You do not abide with me.

3 For You are the Holy One,
   Who abides in the praises of Israel.
4 In You our ancestors trusted;
   they trusted and You set them free.
5 To You they cried out for help and were saved;
   in You they trusted and were not put to shame.

6   But I am a worm, and not a human;
a reproach of the human race,
and the most despicable of the people.

7   All who see me insultingly laugh at me,
they sneer and wag their heads saying:

8   "You trusted in Yahweh, let Yahweh deliver you;
if Yahweh loves you, let Yahweh rescue you!"

9   It was You Who drew me forth from the womb;
and You have been my trust,
since I was upon my mother's breasts.

10 I was put under Your protection from the womb;
and You have been my God since my mother bore me.

11 Be not far from me, for I am in distress,
be near, for I have no one to help me.

12 Fierce enemies like bulls have surrounded me,
mighty enemies of Bashan have besieged me.

13 They opened their mouths on me,
like ravening and roaring lions.

14 I am helpless like water poured out,
all my bones are out of joint;
my heart has become like wax,
melting away within my bosom.

15 My strength is dried up like broken pottery,
and my tongue cleaves to my jaws;
You have thrown me in the dust of death.

16 Vicious enemies like dogs have surrounded me;
a gang of the wicked have enclosed me;
they have pierced my hands and my feet.

17 I can count every one of my bones;
but they stare and gloat over me.

18 They divided my garments among them,
and they cast lots upon my vesture.

19 But You, O Yahweh, be not far from me!
You, my God, hasten to help me!

37

20 Deliver my soul from the sword,
    the one life I have from the paw of the dog!
21 Save me from the mouth of the lion,
    my poor life from the wild bulls' horns!

22 I will tell of Your Name to my kindred;
    in the midst of the assembly I will praise You:
23 You who revere Yahweh, praise God!
    All you children of Israel, glorify God!
    Worship God, all you descendants of Israel!

24 For Yahweh has not despised
    nor disregarded the affliction of the poor.
    Yahweh has not turned away from them,
    but listened when they cried out.

25 My praise shall be of You in the great assembly;
    I will fulfill my vows before those who revere You.
26 The poor shall eat and be satisfied;
    they shall seek and shall praise Yahweh!
    May their hearts live for ever!

27 All the ends of the earth
    shall remember and turn to Yahweh;
    all the families of the nations
    shall worship before You.
28 For dominion belongs to You, Yahweh,
    and You rule over the nations.

29 The proud of the earth shall bow down before You;
    all who go down to the dust shall kneel before You.
30 My soul is alive before You,
    my posterity shall serve You, Yahweh;
    and generations to come shall proclaim Adonai.

31 They shall come and declare Your justice,
    to a people yet unborn,
    and tell all that Yahweh has done.

PSALM 23
Hymn to Yahweh, the Good Shepherd

A Psalm of David.

1 Yahweh is my shepherd,
   I shall not want;

2 You make me rest in green pastures.
   You lead me beside still waters;

3 You restore my spirit.
   You guide me in paths of justice
        for Your Name's sake.

4 Even though I walk through the valley
        with shade dark as death,
   I will fear no evil;
   for You are with me;
   Your rod and Your staff,
        they comfort me.

5 You prepare a table for me
   in the presence of my enemies;
   You anoint my head with oil;
   my cup runs over.

6 Surely Your goodness and mercy
   shall follow me all the days of my life;
   and I shall dwell in Your house
        for all time to come.

PSALM 24
Solemn Entry into the Sanctuary

A Psalm of David.

1 To Yahweh belongs the earth and its fullness,
   the world and all those who dwell in it.

2 You founded it upon the seas,
   and arranged the rivers upon it.

3 Who shall go up to Your mountain, O Yahweh?
  And who shall stand in Your holy place?
4 Those who have clean hands and pure hearts,
  who have not sworn by their souls falsely,
  and have not taken an oath deceitfully.

5 They shall receive blessing from Yahweh,
  and justice from God their Savior.
6 This is the generation of those who seek You,
  who seek Your face, O God of Jacob.

7 Lift up your heads, O you gates!
  and be lifted up, O ancient portals!
  that the glorious Ruler may come in.

8 Who is this glorious Ruler?
  Yahweh, strong and mighty!
  Yahweh, mighty in battle!

9 Lift up your heads, O you gates!
  and be lifted up, O ancient portals!
  that the glorious Ruler may come in.

10 Who is this glorious Ruler?
   Yahweh Sabaoth,
   the Sovereign of glory!

PSALM 25
A Prayer for Guidance and Protection

A Psalm of David.

1 To You, Yahweh, I lift up my soul.
2 O my God, I trust in You,
  do not let me be ashamed;
  and do not let my enemies triumph over me.

3 Let no one who trusts in You be ashamed;
  let the wicked be ashamed with their vanity.

4 Show me Your ways, O Yahweh;
   teach me Your paths.

5 Lead me in Your truth, and teach me,
   for You are my God and my Savior;
   for You I wait all the day long.
6 Remember O Yahweh, Your mercy and faithful love,
   for they are from the beginning of the world.

7 Remember not the sins of my youth, or my offenses;
   but remember me in Your faithful love
   and for Your goodness' sake.
8 You, O Yahweh, are good and just;
   and You show sinners the path of life.

9 You guide the meek in justice,
   and teach the meek Your way.
10 O Yahweh, all Your paths are mercy and truth,
   for those who keep Your covenant and Your decrees.

11 O Yahweh, for Your Name's sake,
   pardon my guilt, for it is great.
12 To those that revere You Yahweh,
   You show the path they should choose.

13 They shall abide in prosperity,
   and their descendants shall inherit the earth.
14 You, O Yahweh, are mindful of those who revere You,
   and You make known to them Your covenant.

15 My eyes are ever toward You, Yahweh,
   for You release my feet from the snare.
16 Turn to me, and be gracious to me;
   for I am lonely and afflicted.

17 Relieve the troubles of my heart,
   and bring me out of my distress.
18 Look upon my affliction and my pain,
   and forgive all my sins.

19 Consider my enemies, for they are many;
    and they hate me with an unjust hatred.
20 Guard my life, and deliver me;
    let me not be ashamed, for I have trusted in You.

21 May integrity and justice preserve me,
    because I wait for You, O Yahweh!
22 Redeem Israel, O God,
    from all its oppressors.

PSALM 26
A Prayer of Confidence in God

A Psalm of David.

1 Do me justice, O Yahweh,
   for I have walked in my integrity;
   and I have trusted in Yahweh
   therefore I shall not waver.

2 Examine me, O Yahweh, and probe me;
   refine my heart and my mind.
3 For Your faithful love is before my eyes,
   and I have walked in faithfulness to You.

4 I have not stayed with evil persons;
   and have not consorted with hypocrites.
5 I have hated the company of evildoers,
   and have not stayed with the wicked.

6 I have washed my hands clean,
   and I have gone around Your altar, O Yahweh,
7 singing aloud a song of thanksgiving,
   and recounting all Your wondrous deeds.

8 O Yahweh, I love the house in which You dwell,
   and the Tabernacle where Your glory dwells.

9 Do not destroy me with sinners,
   nor my life with the violent;

10   whose hands are stained with wickedness,
and whose right hand is full of bribes.

11   But as for me, I walk in my integrity;
save me, and have mercy on me.

12   My foot has stood in the straight path;
in the assemblies I will bless Yahweh.

PSALM 27
A Prayer in Time of Affliction

A Psalm of David.

1   Yahweh is my light and my salvation;
whom shall I fear?
Yahweh is the strength of my life;
of whom shall I be afraid?

2   When evildoers, and my enemies
came at me to devour me,
they stumbled and fell.

3   Though an army should camp against me,
my heart shall not fear.
Though war should rise against me,
in this I will be confident.

4   One thing have I asked of Yahweh,
that I will seek after;
that I may dwell in the house of Yahweh
all the days of my life,
to perceive the loveliness of Yahweh,
and to contemplate in Your temple.

5   For You hide me in Your abode in the day of evil;
You conceal me in the shadow of Your tent,
You set me high upon a rock.

6 And now my head shall be lifted up
above my enemies who have encircled me.
I will offer sacrifices of joy in Your tent.
I will sing and chant praises to Yahweh.

7 Hear, O Yahweh, the sound of my call,
have mercy on me and answer me!
8 My heart says to You, "Seek my face."
"Your face, Yahweh, do I seek."

9 Do not hide Your face from me;
do not turn Your servant away in anger.
You are my help, do not leave me,
do not forsake me, O God my Savior!
10 Though my father and my mother forsake me,
You, Yahweh, will take me up.

11 Yahweh, teach me Your way,
and lead me on the path of justice,
because of those who watch me.
12 Do not deliver me into the hands of my enemies;
for false witnesses have risen against me,
and are breathing out violence.

13 I believe that I shall see
the goodness of Yahweh in the land of the living!
14 Trust in Yahweh, and be of good courage;
let your heart take courage, yes, trust in Yahweh!

PSALM 28
A Hymn of Thanksgiving for Recovery

A Psalm of David.

1 To You I call, O Yahweh, my Rock,
do not be silent to me!
If You stay silent to me,
I become like those who go down to the Pit.

2   Hear the voice of my supplication,
    when I cry to You for help,
    when I lift up my hands
    toward the Holy of Holies in Your temple.

3   Do not count me with the wicked,
    and with the workers of iniquity,
    who speak peace with their neighbors,
    while mischief is in their hearts.

4   Reward them according to their deeds,
    and according to the evil of their practices;
    reward them according to the work of their hands;
    render them their due reward.

5   Because they do not discern Your deeds
    nor the work of Your hands, O Yahweh,
    You strike them down and do not rebuild them.

6   Blessed are You Yahweh!
    for You have heard the voice of my supplications.

7   Yahweh, You are my strength and my shield.
    In You my heart trusts, and I am helped;
    and my heart greatly rejoices,
    and I will praise You with my song.

8   Yahweh, You are the strength of Your people,
    You are the saving refuge of Your anointed.

9   Yahweh, save Your people, bless Your heritage;
    shepherd them, and take care of them for ever.

PSALM 29
A Hymn to Yahweh During a Storm

A Psalm of David.

1   Give to Yahweh, O heavenly beings,
    give to Yahweh glory and honor.

2   Give to Yahweh the glory due the Name;
    worship Yahweh in the majesty of holiness.

45

3   The voice of Yahweh is upon the waters;
    the God of glory thunders;
    Yahweh, is upon countless waters.
4   The voice of Yahweh is powerful;
    the voice of Yahweh is full of majesty.

5   The voice of Yahweh breaks the cedars,
    Yahweh breaks the cedars of Lebanon.
6   Yahweh makes Lebanon to skip like a calf,
    and Sirion like a young wild ox.

7   The voice of Yahweh divides the flames of fire.
8   The voice of Yahweh shakes the wilderness,
    Yahweh shakes the wilderness of Kadesh.
9   The voice of Yahweh makes the hinds to tremble,
    and strips the forests bare.

    In Yahweh's temple all cry, "Glory!"
10 Yahweh sits enthroned over the flood;
    Yahweh sits enthroned as ruler for ever.
11 Yahweh will give strength to the chosen people!
    Yahweh will bless Israel with peace!

PSALM 30
Thanksgiving for Recovery from Sickness

A Psalm of David. A Song at the dedication of the Temple.

1   I will praise You, O Yahweh,
    for You lifted me up,
    and did not let my enemies rejoice over me.

2   O Yahweh my God,
    I cried to You for help, and You healed me.
3   O Yahweh, You brought up my soul from Sheol,
    restored me to life
    from among those gone down to the Pit.

4 "Sing praises to Yahweh, O you faithful ones,
   and give thanks to Yahweh's holy name.
5 For Yahweh's anger lasts but a moment,
   whose favor is for a lifetime.
   Weeping may last for a night,
   but joy comes in the morning.

6 I used to think in my prosperity,
   'I shall never be disturbed.' "
7 By Your favor, O Yahweh,
   You made me strong as a mountain;
   but when You hid Your face, I was troubled.

8 To You, O Yahweh, I call;
   and to You my God, I make my prayer:
9 "What profit is there in shedding my blood,
   in going down to the Pit?
   Would the dust give You praise?
   Would it tell of Your faithfulness?

10 Hear, O Yahweh, and have mercy on me!
    O Yahweh, be my helper!"
11 You turned my mourning into dancing;
    You took off my sackcloth
    and clothed me with joy.

12 Therefore I will sing praise to You
    and not be silent.
    O Yahweh my God,
    I will give thanks to You for ever.

PSALM 31
A Prayer of Trust in God During Illness

To the choir director. A Psalm of David.

1 In You, O Yahweh, I seek refuge;
   let me never be put to shame;
   in Your justice deliver me!

2   Incline Your ear to me, deliver me quickly!
    Be a strong Rock to me,
        a house of refuge to save me!

3   For You are my Rock and my refuge;
    and for Your Name's sake lead me and guide me.
4   Pull me out of the net that they hid for me,
    for You are my protector.
5   Into Your hands I commit my spirit;
    You have redeemed me, O Yahweh, God of truth.

6   I have detested those who worship vain idols;
    but my trust is in Yahweh.
7   I will rejoice and be glad in Your faithful love,
    because You have seen my affliction,
    and have known the distress in my soul.
8   You did not hand me over to the enemy;
    but You gave me freedom to roam at large.

9   Have mercy on me, O Yahweh,
    for I am in distress;
    anguish consumes my eyes,
    and my soul deep within me.
10 For my life is spent with sorrow,
    and my years with sighing;
    my strength fails because of my guilt,
    and my bones are wasted away.

11 I have become a scorn of all my adversaries,
    an object of horror to my neighbors,
    an object of dread to my friends;
    those who see me in the street flee from me.
12 I am forgotten like the unremembered dead,
    I have become like a broken, useless vessel.
13 For I hear the evil report of many
    with terror on every side;
    they scheme together against me,
    and they plot to take my life.

14 But my trust is in You, O Yahweh,
   I say, "You are my God."
15 My destiny is in Your hand, O Yahweh;
   deliver me from the hand of my enemies
   and from those who pursue me.
16 Let Your face shine on Your servant;
   save me in Your faithful love!

17 Let me not be ashamed, O Yahweh,
   for I call on You;
   let the wicked be ashamed,
   let them go to Sheol in silence.
18 Let lying lips be silenced,
   which speak falsely against the just
   with pride and contempt.

19 O how abundant is Your goodness,
   which You have in store for those who revere You,
   and bestow on those who trust in You,
   for all humanity to see!
20 You hide them from human plotting
   in the tabernacle of Your presence;
   You hold them safe under Your shelter
   far from contentious tongues.

21 Blessed be Yahweh,
   for Your wondrous faithful love
   shown me in an entrenched city.
22 I had said in my alarm,
   "I am cut off from Your sight."
   But You heard the sound of my pleading
   when I cried out to You.

23 Love Yahweh, all you holy ones!
   Yahweh preserves the faithful,
   but repays the arrogant with interest.
24 Be strong,
   Yahweh shall make your heart stronger,
   all you who trust in Yahweh!

PSALM 32
Psalm of Thanksgiving for Recovery from Illness: Second Penitential Psalm

A Psalm of David.
A Maskil—An Instruction.

1 Blessed is the one whose sin is forgiven,
  whose offense is blotted out.
2 Blessed is the one
  to whom Yahweh imputes no guilt,
  and in whom there is no guile.

3 Even when I kept silence, my bones wasted away
  from my groaning all day long.
4 For day and night Your hand was heavy upon me;
  my strength was dried up as by the heat of summer.

5 I acknowledged my offense to You,
  and I did not hide my iniquity;
  I said, "I will confess my sins to Yahweh";
  then You forgave the guilt of my sin.

6 Therefore let all the just offer prayer to You,
  when You can be found;
  but when the rush of great waters comes,
  they shall not reach You.
7 You are my place of refuge;
  You preserve me from trouble;
  You surround me with songs of deliverance.

8 I will instruct you
  and show you the way you should go;
  I will counsel you
  and my eye shall be on you.
9 Be not senseless like horses or mules,
  which must be curbed with bit and bridle,
  else they will not come near you.

10   Many are the tribulations of the wicked;
        Yahweh, Your faithful love surrounds
        those who trust in You.
11   Be glad in Yahweh, and rejoice, all you just,
        and shout for joy, all you upright in heart!

PSALM 33
A Hymn to Yahweh, the Creator

1   Rejoice in Yahweh, O you just!
      Praise is becoming to the just.

2   Give thanks to Yahweh with the lyre,
      Sing to Yahweh with a harp of ten strings!
3   Sing to Yahweh a new song,
      play skillfully, with shouts of joy.

4   For the word of Yahweh is just;
      and all Your works are done in truth.
5   You love honesty and justice;
      Your faithful love fills the earth.

6   By the word of Yahweh the heavens were made,
      by the breath of Your mouth all their hosts.
7   You gathered the waters of the sea like a heap;
      You stored away the depths in treasure-houses.

8   Let all the earth revere You, O Yahweh,
      let all who dwell in the world worship You!
9   For You spoke, and it came to be;
      You commanded, and there it stood.

10   Yahweh, You void the plans of the nations;
        You frustrate the plans of the peoples.
11   Yahweh, Your plans stand for ever,
        the thoughts of Your heart to all generations.

12   Blessed is the nation whose God is Yahweh,
        the people whom Yahweh has chosen as heritage!

13 Yahweh, You look down from heaven,
   You see all of the human race.

14 From Your dwelling-place You look
   on all the inhabitants of the earth.
15 You fashioned their hearts
   and observed all their deeds.

16 A ruler is not saved by great force;
   a warrior is not saved by great strength.
17 The war horse is a vain hope for safety,
   for all its strength, it cannot save.

18 Behold, Your eyes, O Yahweh,
   are on those who revere You,
   on those who trust in Your faithful love,
19 that You may deliver their souls from death,
   and keep them alive in famine.

20 Our soul waits for You, Yahweh;
   You are our help and shield.
21 Yes, our heart is glad in You,
   because we trust in Your holy Name.

22 Let Your faithful love, O Yahweh,
   be upon us, even as we trust in You.

PSALM 34
A Psalm of Thanksgiving and Confidence

A Psalm of David, who feigned insanity before Abimelech,
who compelled him to leave.

1 I will bless Yahweh, at all times;
   Whose praise shall ever be on my lips.
2 My soul will glory in Yahweh;
   let the humble hear and rejoice.

3 Glorify Yahweh with me,
   and let us praise God's name together!

4   I sought Yahweh Who answered me,
    and delivered me from all my fears.

5   Look at Yahweh and be filled with light;
    and you will never be humiliated.
6   Yahweh heard the cry of the poor,
    and saved them out of all their troubles.

7   The angel of Yahweh is encamped
    around those who revere God,
    that they may be delivered.
8   Taste and see that Yahweh is good!
    Blessed are those who take refuge in Yahweh!

9   O revere Yahweh, you saints,
    those who revere Yahweh lack for nothing!
10 The rich may grow poor and suffer hunger
    but they who seek Yahweh lack nothing good.

11 Come, O children, listen to me,
    I will teach you the reverence of Yahweh.
12 Where are those who desire life and many days
    that they may see the good time to come?

13 Keep your tongue from evil,
    and your lips from speaking guile.
14 Turn away from evil, and do good;
    seek peace, and pursue it.

15 The eyes of Yahweh are toward the just,
    and Whose ears are open to hear them.
16 But Yahweh's face is set against those who do evil,
    to root out their memory from the earth.

17 When the just cry for help, Yahweh hears,
    and delivers them from all their foes.
18 Yahweh is near to the broken-hearted,
    and saves those crushed in spirit.

19 Many are the afflictions of the just;
    but Yahweh delivers them from them all.

20 Yahweh watches over their bones;
    not one of them shall be broken.

21 Evil brings forth death to the wicked;
    and those who hate the just shall be guilty.
22 The lives of the servants of Yahweh are redeemed
    and none who trusts in Yahweh shall be found guilty.

PSALM 35
A Prayer for Deliverance
from Personal Enemies

A Psalm of David.

1 Plead my cause, O Yahweh,
    with those who strive with me;
    fight against those who fight against me!
2 Take hold of a shield and buckler,
    and stand up for my help!

3 Ready the spear and javelin
    to confront my pursuers!
    Say to my soul, "I am your deliverance!"

4 Let those who seek my life,
    be humiliated and disgraced.
    Let those who plot evil against me,
    be turned back and brought to confusion.

5 Let them be like chaff before the wind,
    with the angel of Yahweh driving them on!
6 Let their way be dark and slippery,
    with the angel of Yahweh pursuing them!

7 Unprovoked they hid their pit-net for me;
    unprovoked they dug a pit for my life.
8 May the pit come upon them unawares!
    May the pit-net which they hid ensnare them;
    let them fall into their own trap!

9 Then my soul shall rejoice
   and exult in Yahweh's deliverance.
10 All my bones shall say,
   "O Yahweh, who is like You,
   You Who rescue the poor
   from those who are too strong for them,
   the weak and the needy
   from those who despoil them?"

11 False witnesses came forward against me;
   they charged me with things I knew not.
12 They rewarded me with evil for good;
   they destroyed my reputation among my people.

13 But I, when they were ill,
   put on a sackcloth,
   afflicted myself with fasting,
   and prayed with head bowed on my bosom,
14 I behaved myself as though
   they had been my friends and my kindred;
   I went about as one bewailing one's parents,
   bowed down and in mourning.

15 During my misery,
   they gathered together and rejoiced;
   strangers whom I knew not
   tore me apart incessantly;
16 with their boasting and mocking,
   they gnashed at me with their teeth.

17 How much longer, Adonai, will You look on?
   Rescue me from their ravages,
   from young lions rescue the one life I have!
18 I will give You thanks in the great assembly;
   I will praise You among many people.

19 Let not my enemies rejoice over me,
   nor the mockers who hate me for no reason
   and wink at me with their eyes.

20 They have no greeting of peace,
    but against the peaceful people of the land,
    they conceive words of deceit.
21 They open wide their mouths against me;
    they say, "Aha, Aha! our eyes have seen it!"

22 Look, O Yahweh; be not silent!
    Adonai, do not stand aloof from me!
23 Bestir Yourself, and awake to my defense,
    see my suffering, my God and Adonai!

24 Vindicate me, as befits Your justice, O Yahweh,
    my God, let them not rejoice over me!
25 Let them not say in their hearts,
    "Aha, this is what we wanted."
    Let them not say, "We have swallowed you up."

26 Let them be put to shame and confusion
    who rejoice at my misfortune.
    Let them be covered with shame and dishonor
    who profit at my expense!

27 Let those who desire my vindication
    shout for joy and be glad,
    and may they ever say, "Great is Yahweh,
    Who desires the well-being of the servant!"
28 Then my tongue will proclaim Your justice
    and all day long Your praise.

PSALM 36
Human Wickedness and Divine Benevolence

To the choir director.
A Psalm of David, the servant of Yahweh.

 1 Perversity inspires the wicked
    within their hearts,
    there is no dread of God
    before their eyes.

2 They see themselves with too flattering an eye,
   to detect or detest their guilt.

3 The words of their mouths are iniquity and deceit;
   they cease to act wisely, to do good.
4 They devise iniquity upon their beds;
   they walk on the path of crime;
   they never shun evil.

5 O Yahweh, Your faithful love is in the heavens,
   Your faithfulness reaches to the clouds.
6 Your justice is like the mountains of God,
   Your judgments are like the great deep;
   O Yahweh, You preserve both humans and beasts.

7 How abundant is Your faithful love, O God!
   Humans take refuge under the shadow of Your wings.
8 They feast on the abundance of Your house,
   and You let them drink from Your delicious springs.
9 For with You is the fountain of life;
   in Your light we shall see light.

10 Maintain Your faithful love to those who know You,
    and Your saving justice to the upright of heart!
11 Let not the foot of arrogance come against me,
    nor the hand of the wicked drive me away.
12 See how the evildoers have fallen;
    they are thrust down, unable to rise.

PSALM 37
Reflections on Good and Evil

A Psalm of David.

1 Do not be outraged about the wicked,
   or be resentful over those who do wrong!
2 For they will soon vanish like the grass,
   and wither like the green of the fields.

3 Put your trust in Yahweh, and do good;
   that you may dwell in the land, and live secure.
4 Take your delight in Yahweh,
   and Yahweh will grant you your heart's requests.

5 Commit your destiny to Yahweh;
   trust in Yahweh, who acts on your behalf.
6 Yahweh will bring forth your justice like the light,
   your pardon as bright as the noonday.

7 Be still before Yahweh, and wait patiently;
   Do not brood over those who prosper on their way,
   over those who succeed by devious means.

8 Refrain from anger, forsake indignation!
   Do not be outraged, it can only harm you.
9 For the evildoers shall be cut off;
   but those who wait for Yahweh,
   they shall inherit the earth.

10 A little while, and the wicked will be no more;
    and if you look for their place,
    it shall no longer be there.
11 But the meek shall inherit the earth,
    and delight themselves in abundant peace.

12 The wicked plot against the just,
    and gnash their teeth at them;
13 but Adonai laughs at their efforts,
    knowing that their end is in sight.

14 The wicked have drawn out the sword
    and have arched their bows,
    to bring down the poor and needy,
    to destroy those who walk uprightly.
15 Their sword shall pierce their own heart,
    and their bows shall be broken.

16 The little that the just has is better,
    than the great wealth of the wicked.

17 The arms of the wicked shall be shattered;
    while Yahweh sustains the just.

18 Yahweh watches over the lives of the good,
    and their heritage will endure for ever;
19 they are not put to shame in bad times,
    in time of famine they will have plenty.

20 But the wicked shall perish;
    the enemies of Yahweh shall be consumed
    like the green of the pasture;
    more quickly than smoke they shall vanish.

21 The wicked borrows, and never repays;
    but the just is gracious in giving.
22 Those who are blessed by Yahweh,
    shall inherit the earth,
    but those cursed by Yahweh
    shall be annihilated.

23 Yahweh guides our steps
    and keeps them firm upon the way,
    the way in which Yahweh takes delight.
24 Though the just may fall,
    they shall not be hurt,
    for Yahweh upholds their hands.

25 I have been young, and now am grown old;
    yet I have not seen the just forsaken
    or their children begging bread.
26 They are always generous in lending
    and their children become a blessing.

27 Turn away from evil, and do good;
    that you may live for ever.
28 For Yahweh loves justice;
    and will not forsake the faithful ones.

    For ever they shall be safeguarded,
    but the descendants of the wicked
    shall be annihilated.

29 The just shall inherit the earth,
    and dwell upon it for ever.

30 The mouths of the just announce wisdom,
    and their tongue proclaims justice.
31 The law of their God is in their hearts;
    their steps do not slide.

32 The wicked lie in wait for the just,
    and seek to destroy them.
33 Yahweh will not abandon them to their power,
    or let them be condemned when brought to trial.

34 Trust in Yahweh, and be faithful,
    you will be exalted.
    You will inherit the earth,
    and will see the destruction of the wicked.

35 I have seen the wicked thriving,
    and flourishing like the cedars of Lebanon.
36 They passed by and were no more;
    though I sought them, they could not be found.

37 Observe the virtuous, and behold the just,
    for there is a good end for the peace-loving.
38 But sinners shall be destroyed altogether;
    the end of the wicked shall be destruction.

39 The deliverance of the just is from Yahweh;
    Yahweh is their refuge in time of trouble.
40 Yahweh helps them and rescues them;
    Yahweh rescues them from the wicked,
    and saves them, because they trust in God.

PSALM 38
A Lament in Time of Distress:
Third Penitential Psalm

A Psalm of David, for the memorial offering.

1 O Yahweh, do not rebuke me in Your anger,
  nor punish me in Your wrath!
2 For Your arrows have pierced deep into me,
  and Your hand presses heavily on me.
3 There is no soundness in my flesh
  because of Your indignation;
  there is no health in my bones
  because of my sin.

4 For my iniquities overwhelm me;
  they weigh like a burden too heavy for me.
5 My wounds grow stinking and swelling,
  because of my senselessness.
6 My body is bent and torn with pain;
  all day long I go in mourning.

7 My limbs are filled with inflammation,
  there is no wholeness in my flesh.
8 I feel burnt out and utterly crushed;
  I groan in the distress of my heart.

9 Adonai, all my longing is known to You,
  my sighing is not hidden from You.
10 My heart trembles, my strength fails me;
  and as for the light of my eyes,
  it also has gone from me.

11 My friends and companions shun my plague,
  even the dearest of them keep their distance.
12 Those who seek my life lay their snares,
  they who desire my misfortune, speak of violence,
  and contemplate deception all the day long.

13 I do not hear, as though I were deaf;
    like a mute who is unable to speak.
14 I am like one who does not hear,
    and in whose mouth there is no reproach.

15 But for You, O Yahweh, do I wait;
    it is You, Adonai my God, who will answer.
16 For I pray, "Let them not rejoice over me,
    let them not ridicule me, when my feet waver!"

17 For I am prepared to suffer,
    and my affliction is before me always.
18 I acknowledge my sinfulness,
    I am sorry for my sins.

19 My enemies are strong and alert;
    many are those who hate me wrongfully.
20 They reward me evil for good;
    they reproach me for trying to do good.

21 Do not forsake me, O Yahweh!
    O my God, be not far from me!
22 Make haste to help me,
    Adonai, my Deliverer!

PSALM 39
A Prayer for Healing from a Serious Sickness

To the choir director: to Jeduthun. A Psalm of David.

1 I said, "I will guard my expressions,
    that I may not sin with my tongue;
    I will constrain my mouth,
    so long as the wicked are in my presence."
2 I was mute and was still,
    I was silent, even from the good,
    and my sufferings grew worse.

3 My heart had been smoldering within me,
    and as I thought of it, it flared up,
    then I spoke out with my tongue:

4 "Yahweh, let me know my destiny,
   and for how much longer I have to live;
   let me know how fleeting my life is!

5 Behold, You have made my days a short span,
   and my lifetime is as nothing in Your sight.
   Human beings are like a mere puff of breath!
6 Human beings go about like a shadow!
   they disappear like a puff of breath;
   they heap up, and do not know who will gather!

7 And now, Adonai, what am I to hope for?
   My hope is in You.
8 Deliver me from all my transgressions.
   Do not set me forth as the reproach of the fool!
9 I am speechless, I do not open my mouth;
   for it is You Who have done it.

10 Remove Your scourge from me;
   I am worn out by the blows of Your hand.
11 When You chastise us with rebukes for our sins,
   You consume like a moth what is dear to us;
   surely every one is a mere puff of breath!

12 Hear my prayer, O Yahweh,
   and listen to my cry for help;
   Do not remain silent at my tears!
   For I am a passing guest in Your house,
   a sojourner, like all my ancestors.
13 O rescue me, that I may rest in peace,
   before I pass away and be no more!"

PSALM 40
A Hymn of Thanksgiving for Healing

To the choir director. A Psalm of David.

1 I waited patiently for You, Yahweh;
   and You turned to me and heard my cry.

2   You drew me up from the desolate pit,
    out of the miry clay,
    and set my feet upon a rock,
    making my steps secure.

3   You put a new song in my mouth,
    a song of praise to You, our God.
    Many will see and rejoice,
    and put their trust in You, Yahweh.

4   Blessed are those
    who put their trust in Yahweh,
    who do not turn to idolatry,
    and who do not go after falsehood!

5   Many are the wonders You have done for us,
    O Yahweh our God,
    and wonderful is Your care for us!
    Were I to proclaim and tell them,
    they would be too numerous to number.
    There is no one like You.

6   Sacrifice and offering You do not desire;
    but as for me, I now understand:
    burnt offering and sin offering You did not require.

7   Then I said, "Here I am, I come;
    in the beginning of the books,
    it is written of me;
8   My delight is to do Your will, O my God;
    Your law is deep within my heart."

9   I have announced Your saving justice
    in the great assembly;
    and as You know, O Yahweh,
    I did not restrain my lips.

10 I have not concealed Your saving help in my heart,
    I have spoken of Your faithfulness and salvation;

I have not hidden Your faithful love and truth
from the great assembly.

11 Do not withhold, O Yahweh
Your compassion from me,
Your faithful love and faithfulness
will always preserve me!

12 For innumerable are the evils that surround me;
my sins have overtaken me that I cannot see my way;
they outnumber the hairs of my head;
and my heart fails me.

13 Be pleased, O Yahweh, to rescue me!
O Yahweh, please continue to help me!

14 Let all of them be put to shame and confusion
who seek to snatch away my life;
let them be driven backward
and put to shame who desire my ruin!

15 Let them be dismayed in their shame
who say to me, "Aha, Aha!"

16 But may all who seek You
rejoice and be glad in You;
may those who love Your deliverance
say constantly, "Yahweh be glorified!"

17 Though I am poor and needy,
Adonai will think of me.
You are my helper and my deliverer;
do not delay, O my God!

PSALM 41
A Prayer of Thanksgiving for Recovery
of Health

To the choir director. A Psalm of David.

1 Blessed are those who look after the poor!
Yahweh delivers them in the time of trouble;

2 Yahweh protects them and keeps them alive;
   calls them blessed upon the earth,
   and does not abandon them
   to the pleasure of their enemies.
3 Yahweh sustains them on their sickbed;
   and heals all their infirmities.

4 Once I said, "O Yahweh, be gracious to me;
   restore me, though I have sinned against You!"
5 My enemies asked me in malice:
   "When will you die, and your name perish?"
6 When people come to see me,
   they speak without sincerity,
   while their heart devises evil;
   when they go out, they gossip about me.

7 All who hate me whisper together about me,
   and maintain I deserve the misery I suffer.
8 A fatal sickness has a grip on me, they say,
   and now that I lie in bed sick,
   I will not rise again from where I lie.
9 Even my trusted friend in whom I relied,
   who ate of my bread, has betrayed me.

10 But You, O Yahweh, be gracious to me,
   and raise me up, that I may settle with them!
11 By this I know that You are pleased with me,
   because my enemy has not triumphed over me.
12 You have upheld me in my integrity,
   and set me in Your presence for ever.

13 Blessed be Yahweh, the God of Israel,
   from eternity to eternity! Amen and Amen.

BOOK TWO
Psalms 42-72

PSALM 42
The Prayer of Longing for Yahweh: Part 1

To the choir director.
A Maskil—An Instruction of the Korahites.

1   As a deer longs for watering springs,
    so for You, O God, my soul longs.

2   My soul thirsts for God, the living God;
    when shall I come to behold Your face, O God?

3   My tears have been my food night and day,
    while they said to me day after day,
    "Where is your God?"

4   As I pour out my soul before God in distress,
    I remember those times
    when I went with the crowds,
    and led them in procession to the house of God,
    amid shouts of joy and songs of thanksgiving,
    with the multitude keeping festival.

5   Why are you so depressed, O my soul,
    and why do you moan within me?
    Hope in God; I shall always thank you,
    my Savior, my Presence and my God.

6   My soul is depressed within me,
    because I remember You from the land of Jordan
    and from the Hermons, from Mount Mizar.

7   Deep calls to deep at the sound of Your waterfalls;
    all Your waves and Your billows are gone over me.

8   By day You, Yahweh, bestow faithful love;
    and at night You fill me with Your song,
    a prayer to my living God.

9   I shall say to God, my Rock:
    "Why have You forgotten me?
    Why must I go about in mourning
    with the enemy harassing me?"

10 As with a deadly wound in my body,
    my adversaries reproach me,
    while they say to me all day long,
    "Where is your God?"

11 Why are you so depressed, O my soul,
    and why do you moan within me?
    Hope in God; I shall always thank you,
    my Savior, my Presence and my God.

PSALM 43
The Prayer of Longing for Yahweh: Part 2

1   Do me justice, O God,
    defend my cause against the ungodly people,
    from the deceitful and the unjust deliver me.

2   For You, O God, are my refuge;
    why have You rejected me?
    Why must I go about in mourning
    with the enemy harassing me?

3   Send forth Your light and Your truth;
    let them lead me on,
    let them bring me to Your holy mountain,
    to the place where You dwell!

4   Then will I go to the altar of God,
    God of my joy and delight;
    then will I praise You with the lyre,
    O God, my God.

5 Why are you so depressed, O my soul,
and why do you moan within me?
Hope in God; I shall always thank you,
my Savior, my Presence and my God.

PSALM 44
A Community Prayer for Deliverance
from Enemies

To the choir director.
A Maskil—An Instruction of the Korahites.

1 O God, we have heard with our own ears,
we have been told by our ancestors,
the deeds You did in their days,
in days of old Your hand worked wonders.

2 You rooted nations out with Your own hand,
to plant Your people on the land,
You dispersed the peoples of the land,
to make room for Your own people.

3 They did not seize the land with their swords,
nor did their own arm make them victorious;
but it was Your arm, Your right hand,
and the light of Your face;
since You favored them.

4 You are my Ruler, my God,
Who decreed the victories of Jacob.
5 Through You we struck down our adversaries;
through Your Name we trampled our assailants.

6 For I will not trust in my bow,
and my sword will not save me.
7 From our enemies You have saved us,
and have put to shame those who hate us.
8 We gloried in God day by day,
and for ever we will praise Your Name.

69

9   But now You have cast us off and disgraced us,
    You no longer go forth with our armies.
10 You have made us retreat from our foes;
    and our enemies despoiled us as they please.

11 You have given us up like sheep for food,
    and have scattered us among the nations.
12 You have sold Your people for no gain,
    You are not increased by their price.

13 You have made us a disgrace to our neighbors,
    a mockery and a scorn to those around us.
14 You have made us a byword among the nations,
    a laughingstock among the peoples.

15 My disgrace is continually before me,
    and shame of my face covers me,
16 at the sound of insult and abuse,
    at the sight of the avenger and the foe.

17 All this has come upon us,
    though we have not forgotten You,
    or been disloyal to Your covenant.
18 Our heart has not turned away,
    nor have our feet strayed from Your way.
19 Yet You have crushed us in the place of jackals,
    and covered us over with shade dark as death.

20 If we had forgotten the name of our God,
    and stretched out our hands to an alien god;
21 would not God have found this out,
    You, Who know the secrets of the heart?
22 For Your sake we are being slain all day long,
    and we are counted as sheep for slaughter.

23 Awake Adonai! Why are You asleep?
    Awake! Do not cast us off for ever!
24 Why do You turn Your face away,
    forgetting our affliction and distress?

25 For our souls are bowed down to the dust;
    our bodies are pressed to the ground.
26 Arise! come to our help!
    Deliver us as befits Your faithful love!

PSALM 45
A Royal Wedding Song

To the choir director: to the tune of "Lilies."
A Maskil—An Instruction of the Korahites; a love song.

1 My heart overflows with a sweet melody;
   as I sing my verses to the king;
   my tongue is like the pen of a ready scribe.

2 You are the fairest of all humans;
   grace is poured out upon your lips;
   thus God has blessed you for ever.
3 Gird your sword upon your thigh,
   prevail in your glory and majesty!

4 Ride forth victoriously in your majesty
   for the cause of truth, meekness and justice,
   let your right hand show forth awesome deeds!
5 Your arrows are sharp,
   the peoples fall under your feet,
   your enemies lose heart.

6 Eternal and everlasting God has enthroned you!
   Your royal scepter is a scepter of justice.
7 You love justice and detest wickedness;
   therefore God, your God, has anointed you
   with the oil of gladness above all your rivals.

8 With myrrh, aloes and cassia your robes are fragrant;
   from ivory palaces you are greeted with string music.
9 Royal princes are in your retinue,
   the queen stands at your right hand in gold of Ophir.

10 Listen, my daughter, and consider my words;
     forget your people and your ancestral home.
11 Since the one who falls in love with your beauty
     is your king you shall render homage.

12 The people of Tyre will court your favor with gifts,
     the richest of the nations with their wealth.
13 The royal princess is all glorious within
     and she is bedecked in gold-woven robes.

14 She shall be led to the king, in embroidered robes
     with her companions, the virgins, in her train.
15 With joy and gladness they shall be led along,
     and shall enter the palace of the king.

16 In place of your ancestors shall be your children;
     you will make them rulers in all the earth.
17 I will sing your name through all generations,
     and the peoples will praise you for ever and ever.

PSALM 46
Hymn to God, Our Refuge and Strength

To the choir director.
A Psalm of the Korahites.
According to Alamoth. A Song.

1 God is our refuge and strength,
    an ever-present help in time of trouble.
2 So we will not be afraid should the earth shake,
    should the mountains slide into the heart of the sea;
3 should its waters roar and foam,
    should the mountains tremble in its swelling.

     (Yahweh Sabaoth is with us;
     the God of Jacob is our refuge.)

4 There is a river
    whose streams gladden the city of God,
    the holy habitation of the Most High.

5 God is in its midst, it shall not be toppled;
   God will help it at the break of dawn.
6 The nations rage, the dominions totter;
   at God's voice, the earth melts away.

7 Yahweh Sabaoth is with us;
   the God of Jacob is our refuge.

8 Come, observe the works of Yahweh,
   Who has put fertility in the earth,
9 Who causes wars to cease to the end of the earth,
   breaks the bow, and shatters the spear,
   and burns the war-chariots in the fire!
10 "Be still, and know that I am God.
   I am exalted above the nations,
   I am exalted above the earth!"

11 Yahweh Sabaoth is with us;
   the God of Jacob is our refuge.

PSALM 47
A Hymn to Yahweh, Sovereign of All Nations

To the choir director.
A Psalm of the Korahites.

1 Clap your hands, all you peoples!
   Shout aloud to God with songs of joy!
2 For Yahweh, the Most High, the Awesome,
   is a great ruler over all the earth.

3 Yahweh humbled peoples in our sight,
   and subdued the nations.
4 Yahweh has chosen our inheritance for us:
   the glory of beloved Israel.

5 God mounts the throne amid shouts of joy,
   Yahweh with the sound of a trumpet.
6 Sing praise to God, sing praise!
   Sing praise to our Ruler, sing praise!

7 For God is the Ruler of all the earth;
  sing a psalm for edification.
8 God reigns over the nations;
  God sits on the throne of Holiness.

9 The leaders of the nations assemble
  with the people of the God of Abraham.
  The shields of the earth belong to God,
  Who is exceedingly exalted.

PSALM 48
Song of Zion, the Mountain of God

A Song. A Psalm of the Korahites.

1 Great is Yahweh and most worthy of praise,
  in the city of our God, God's Holy mountain.
2 Beautiful on high, the joy of all the earth,
  is Mount Zion, in the heart of the north,
  the city of the great Ruler.
3 God is in its citadels
  and is its sure defense.

4 For behold, the rulers made alliance,
  together they advanced.
5 They saw and were astounded,
  they panicked and fled away.
6 Trembling seized them on the spot,
  pains like those of a woman in labor.

7 As though a wind from the east,
  You shattered the ships of Tarshish.
8 As we have heard, so have we seen
  in the city of Yahweh Sabaoth,
  in the city of our God,
  which God has established for ever.

9 We reflect on Your faithful love,
  in the midst of Your temple, O God.

10 Both Your Name and Your Praise O God,
reach to the ends of the earth.
Your right hand is full of generosity.
11 Mount Zion shall be joyful,
the cities of Judah shall rejoice,
because of Your saving justice!

12 Walk around Zion, go all around it,
yes, count the towers thereof.
13 Admire its magnitude, examine its fortresses,
that you may tell it to future generations.
14 For this is our God for ever,
for ever our guide.

PSALM 49
The Futility of Worldly Possessions

To the choir director.
A Psalm of the Korahites.

1 Hear this, all nations!
listen, all who dwell on earth,
2 people of lowly and lofty birth,
both rich and poor alike!

3 My mouth shall speak wisdom;
my heart shall proclaim prudence.
4 I will incline my ear to a proverb;
I will chant my riddle upon the harp.

5 Why should I be afraid in times of trouble,
when I am beset by the malice of my foes?
6 They trust in their possessions
and boast of the abundance of their wealth.

7 Truly one can never redeem oneself,
or pay to God one's own ransom price.
8 Too high is the ransom for one's life,
and one would never have enough.

9   You shall live for ever,
    and not see corruption ever.

10 Yes, you will see that even the wise die,
    the fool and the witless pass away likewise,
    and leave their wealth behind to others.
11 For ever their graves are their homes,
    their dwelling-place to all generations,
    though they call lands after their own names.

12 In prosperity people lose their good sense,
    they become like the beasts that cease to be.
13 This is the fate of those who trust in fortune,
    the end of those who indulged in their taste.

14 They are penned in Sheol like sheep,
    Death shall be their shepherd,
    the upright shall rule over them.
    The grave shall soon consume their beauty
    and Sheol shall be their home.
15 But God will surely ransom my soul,
    will snatch me up from the clutches of Sheol.

16 Be not concerned when others become rich,
    when the wealth of their houses increases.
17 For when they die, nothing will they take with them;
    their wealth will not go down with them.

18 They counted themselves happy, while living,
    for people praise you when you do well for yourself.
19 They will go to the generation of their ancestors,
    they shall not see light for ever.
20 In prosperity people lose their good sense,
    they become like the beasts that cease to be.

PSALM 50
Hymn to Yahweh God, the Divine Judge

A Psalm of Asaph.

1 Yahweh God, the Mighty One has spoken
   summoning the earth from east to west.
2 Out of Zion, perfection of beauty,
   God shines forth.

3 Our God is coming and will not be silent,
   before Whom is a devouring fire,
   round about whom a mighty tempest.
4 God shall summon the heavens above,
   and the earth to judge the people:

5 "Gather to me my faithful ones,
   who sealed my covenant with sacrifice!
6 The heavens declare my justice,
   for I am the God of justice!"

7 "Hear, O my people, and I will speak,
   I will testify against you, O Israel!
   I am God, your God.
8 Not for your sacrifices do I reprove you,
   yes, your burnt offerings are ever before me.
9 I will not accept any bull from your homes,
   nor a single goat from your folds.
10 For every animal of the forest is mine,
   and the cattle on a thousand hills.

11 I know every bird in the air,
   and all that moves in the field is mine.
12 Were I hungry, I would not tell you;
   since the world and all it holds is mine.
13 Do I eat the flesh of bulls,
   or drink the blood of goats?

14 Offer to God thanksgiving as a sacrifice
   and fulfill the vows you make to the Most High;

15 and then if you call upon me in time of trouble;
I will deliver you, and you shall glorify me."

16 But to the wicked God says:
"What right have you to recite my statutes,
to take my covenant on your lips?

17 For you detest my instruction,
and cast my words behind your back.

18 You join with a thief when you see one,
and throw in your lot with adulterers.

19 You give your mouth free rein for evil,
and your tongue frames deceit.

20 You sit and speak against your kindred;
you slander your own mother's child.

21 These things you do, am I to remain silent?
Do you think that I am really one like yourself.
But now I will rebuke you,
and accuse you before your face.

22 Now think of this, you who forget God,
lest I rend you with none to rescue!

23 Those who bring thanksgiving as sacrifice honor me;
to those whose ways are just,
I will show the salvation of God!"

PSALM 51
A Prayer of Contrition:
Fourth Penitential Psalm

To the choir director.
A Psalm of David, when Nathan the prophet came to him,
after he had gone in to Bathsheba.

1 Have mercy on me, O God, in Your faithful love,
in Your great compassion wipe away my offenses.

2 Wash me thoroughly from my guilt,
and cleanse me from my sin!

3 For I acknowledge my offenses,
   and my sin is constantly before me.
4 'Against You, against You alone, have I sinned,
   and I did that which is evil in Your sight.'

   You always show justice in Your sentence
   and are without reproach when You judge.
5 Indeed, I was born with guilt of sin,
   a sinner from the moment of conception.

6 Behold, You desire sincerity of heart,
   and secretly teach me wisdom in my heart.
7 Cleanse me with hyssop, and I shall be clean;
   wash me, and I shall be purer than snow.

8 Let me hear songs of joy and gladness,
   and the bones You have crushed will dance.
9 Turn Your face away from my sins,
   and wipe away all my guilt.

10 Create in me a clean heart, O God,
   recreate within me a faithful spirit.
11 Do not banish me from Your presence,
   nor deprive me of Your Spirit of holiness.

12 Restore to me the joy of Your salvation,
   and sustain in me a generous spirit.
13 Then I will teach wrongdoers Your ways,
   and sinners will return to Your presence.

14 Deliver me from death, O God, my saving God,
   and my tongue, will loudly sing Your justice.
15 Adonai, open my lips,
   and my mouth will proclaim Your praise.

16 You do not desire a sacrifice, were I to give it,
   nor do You delight in a holocaust.
17 My sacrifice, O God, is a broken spirit;
   a broken and contrite heart, You will not reject.

18 In Your graciousness do good to Zion,
    rebuild the walls of Jerusalem.
19 Then You will be pleased with sacrifices of justice,
    with holocausts and whole offerings;
    then they shall offer bulls on Your altar.

PSALM 52
The Destiny of the Wicked: A Reflection

To the choir director.
A Maskil—An Instruction of David, when Doeg, the
Edomite, came and told Saul, "David has come to the
house of Ahimelech."

1 Why do you boast of wickedness, O champion?
   Why, O false devotee of God,
2 all day long, do you plot destruction?
   Your tongue is like a sharp razor,
   you worker of deception.

3 You love evil more than good,
   lying more than telling the truth.
4 You love all words that destroy,
   O deceitful tongue.

5 That is why God will crush you,
   destroy you once and for all,
   snatch you away from your tent;
   uproot you from the land of the living.

6 The just shall look on with awe,
   and shall laugh at you and say:
7 "See someone who would not make God a refuge,
   but trusted in the abundance of riches,
   and sought refuge in wealth!"

8 But I, like a green olive tree
   in the house of God,
   put my trust in God's faithful love
   for ever and ever.

9   I shall praise You, O Eternal,
for what You have done.
I shall proclaim in Your Name, O Goodness,
in the presence of Your devoted ones.

PSALM 53
The Destiny of the Foolish: A Reflection

To the choir director: to the tune of "Mahalath."
A Maskil—An Instruction of David.

1   Fools say in their hearts,
"There is no God."
They commit corrupt, hateful deeds;
there is no one who does good.

2   God looks down from heaven
upon all the human race
to see if there be anyone wise,
anyone who searches for God.

3   Everyone has become unfaithful;
together they are all depraved;
there is not one that does good,
not a single one.

4   They no longer recognize evil;
they consume my people like bread;
they have no respect for God.

5   There they are, in great affliction,
in affliction such as has not been!
God will scatter the bones of the wicked;
for rejected by God, they will be humiliated.

6   Who will bring deliverance to Israel from Zion?
When God restores the fortunes of the people,
Jacob shall rejoice and Israel shall be glad.

PSALM 54
Confident Prayer for Deliverance
from Enemies

To the choir director: with stringed instruments.
A Maskil—An Instruction of David, when the Ziphites
went and told Saul, "David is in hiding among us."

1 Save me, O God, by Your Name,
and by Your might defend me.
2 O God, hear my prayer,
to the words of my mouth, give ear.

3 For strangers have risen up against me,
tyrants seek my life;
they have disregarded You, O God.

4 Behold, God is my helper;
You, Adonai, are my life sustainer.
5 You avenge my enemies with evil;
and silence them with Your truth.

6 I will offer You fitting sacrifice, O Yahweh;
I will praise Your Name, for its goodness.
7 For You have delivered me out of all troubles,
and my eye has seen the defeat of my enemies.

PSALM 55
Complaint against Disloyal Companions

To the choir director: with stringed instruments.
A Maskil—An Instruction of David.

1 Give ear, O God, to my prayer;
and do not hide Yourself from my cry!
2 Heed me, and answer me;
return to my cry and incline to me.

3 I shudder at the enemy's shouts,
at the outcry of the wicked;
they bring charges against me,
in anger they savor enmity against me.

4 My heart is in anguish within me,
   the terrors of death have fallen upon me.
5 Fear and trembling have come upon me,
   and the shadow of death overwhelms me.

6 I said: "O that I had wings like a dove!
   then I would fly away and be at rest;
7 I would take flight far away,
   in the wilderness would I settle.

8 To my shelter I would hasten,
   out of the rushing wind and tempest."
9 Destroy, Adonai, their forked tongues,
   for I see violence and strife in the city.

10 They go around it on its walls day and night,
   injustice and wickedness are in its midst.
11 Corruption lives in its midst;
   tyranny and deceit are for ever in its streets.

12 If it were an enemy who insulted me
      —then I could have borne it;
   if it were an adversary who defamed me
      —then I could have hidden.

13 But it was you, a person of my own rank,
   my companion, and my dear friend,
14 you, with whom I shared intimate friendship,
   with whom I marched in procession into God's house.

15 Let death come upon them;
   let them go down to Sheol alive;
   let evil go down with them into their graves.
16 As for me, I will call upon God;
   and Yahweh will deliver me.

17 At evening and in the morning and at noon
   I will grieve and moan,
   and the Deliverer will hear my voice.

18 And will give me freedom and peace
    from those who wage war against me,
    for many there are who oppose me.

19 God will hear and answer me,
    the Eternal One will humble them,
    because there are no changes in them,
    and because they do not revere God.

20 They attack those at peace with them,
    and have broken their covenant.
21 Though their speech is smoother than butter,
    yet enmity is in their hearts;
    their words are more delicate than oil,
    yet they are sharper than swords.

22 Surrender your burdens onto Yahweh,
    and Yahweh will sustain you,
    and will never allow the just to stumble.

23 But You, O God, will toss them down
    to the abyss of destruction.
    The bloodthirsty and the deceitful ones
    shall not live out half their days.
    As for me, I put my trust in You.

PSALM 56
A Prayer of Reliance on God, the Provider

To the choir director:
to the tune of "The Dove on Far-off Terebinths."
A Miktam of David, when the Philistines seized him in Gath.

1 Have mercy on me, O God,
   for my enemies trample upon me,
   all day long they oppress me.
2 My enemies hound me all day long,
   countless they are who rise against me.

3 O Most High, when I have fears,
   I will put my trust in You.
4 In Your promises, O God, do I boast,
   in You I put my trust and have no fear,
   what can mortal foes do against me?

5 All day long my slanderers vex me,
   and they devise evil against me.
6 They league together and lie in wait,
   they lie in wait and watch my steps;
   they watch and wait to take my life.

7 Should they be rewarded for their crimes?
   In Your anger reject them, O God,
   and count them with the nations!

8 You have kept count of my laments;
   You put my tears in Your bottle!
   Are they not listed in Your book?
9 Then my enemies will be turned back
   in the day when I call on You.

   This I know, for God is with me.
10 In Your promises, O God, do I boast,
   In Your promises, O Yahweh, do I boast.
11 In God I put my trust and have no fear,
   what can mortals do against me?

12 My vows to You I will fulfill, O God;
   I will render to You thank offerings.
13 For You have delivered my life from death,
   and my steps from stumbling,
   that I may walk pleasing in Your sight,
   O God, in the land of the living.

PSALM 57
Confident Prayer in Time of Danger

To the choir director: to the tune of "Do Not Destroy."
A Miktam of David, when he fled from Saul, in the cave.

1   Have mercy on me, O God, have mercy on me,
for in You my soul takes refuge,
in the shadow of Your wings I will take refuge,
until the storms of calamity pass by me.

2   I call to You, God the Most High,
to You, God Who have done everything for me.

3   Send help from heaven and save me,
put to shame those who trample upon me.

4   O God, send forth Your mercy and truth!
I lie surrounded by lions,
yearning for human prey;
their teeth are spears and arrows,
their tongues sharp swords.

5   Be exalted, O God, above the heavens!
Let Your glory be over all the earth!

6   They spread a net for my feet,
my soul was bowed down.
They dug a pit ahead of me,
may they themselves fall into it.

7   My heart is ready, O God,
my heart is ready!
I will sing and make melody!

8   Awake, my honor!
Awake, O harp and lyre!
I will awake the dawn with praise!

9   I will praise You, Adonai, among the peoples,
I will sing to Your Name among the nations.

10 For Your faithful love towers to the heavens,
Your faithfulness to the clouds.

11   Be exalted, O God, above the heavens!
     Let Your glory be over all the earth!

PSALM 58
Psalmist's Imprecations against Unjust Judges

To the choir director: to the tune of "Do Not Destroy."
A Miktam of David.

1   Do you indeed pronounce justice in silence?
    Do you judge people justly?
2   No, you devise injustice in your hearts,
    you deal out violence with your hands.

3   The wicked have gone astray since the womb,
    liars, they have been since their birth.
4   They have venom like the venom of a serpent,
    and are deaf like an adder that blocks its ears,
5   so as not to hear the voice of charmers,
    the skillful casters of spells.

6   O God, rip their teeth in their mouths;
    knock out the fangs of these young lions, O Yahweh!
7   May they drain away like water running to waste;
    like cut grass let them be trampled and wither.
8   Let them disappear like the snail into slime,
    like a stillborn child that never sees the sun.

9   Sooner than your pots can feel the heat of thorns,
    whether green or ablaze, may they be swept away!
10 The just will rejoice when they see vengeance done;
    they will bathe their feet in the blood of the wicked.
11 People will say, "There is a reward for the just;
    Yes, there is a God to dispense justice on earth."

PSALM 59
Psalmist's Imprecations against Slanders

To the choir director: to the tune of "Do Not Destroy."
A Miktam of David, when Saul sent soldiers to watch
David's house in order to kill him.

1 Rescue me from my enemies, O my God,
    against my attackers be my bulwark.
2 Rescue me from the evil-doers,
    and save me from the murderers.

3 They lie in wait for my life;
    mighty ones conspire against me,
    for no offense, O Yahweh, no sin of mine.
4 For no guilt of mine,
    they hurry and take up arms against me.

    Be attentive, O Yahweh, and stand by me!
5 You, God of Sabaoth, are God of Israel.
    Rise up to punish all the nations;
    be not merciful to these malicious traitors.

6 They wait till the nightfall,
    to howl like dogs prowling about the city.
7 There they are, bellowing with their mouths,
    and snarling with their lips,
    they murmur, "Who is there to hear us?"

8 But You, O Yahweh, shall laugh at them;
    You hold the nations in derision.
9 O my Strength, I will sing Your praises;
    for You, O God, are my Fortress.

10 O my gracious God, will You come to my help?
    O God, will You let me gloat over my foes?
11 Slay them, lest my people falter;
    scatter them by Your power,
    bring them down, Adonai, our shield!

12 For the sin of their mouths,
    the gossip of their lips,
    the cursing and lies which they utter,
    let them be trapped in their conceit.

13 Destroy them in Your anger,
    destroy them till they are no more,
    that they may know that God is Ruler
    in Jacob to the ends of the universe.

14 They wait till the nightfall,
    to howl like dogs prowling about the city.

15 They roam up and down for food,
    and growl if they are not satisfied.

16 But I will sing of Your Strength,
    I will sing of Your mercy in the morning;
    for You have been to me a fortress,
    and a refuge in the day of my distress.

17 To You, O my Strength, I will sing praises
    for You, O God, are my fortress,
    the God Who loves me with faithful love.

PSALM 60
National Lament after Defeat

To the choir director: to the tune of "Lily of the Testimony."
A Miktam of David; for instruction; when he strove with
Aram-naharaim and with Aram-zobah, and when Joab on his
return killed twelve thousand of Edom in the Valley of Salt.

1 O God, You have rejected us, scattered us
   You were angry, do not turn away from us.

2 You have made the earth tremble, split it open
   now mend its rifts, for it stumbles.

3 You have made Your people feel hardship;
   You have made us drink the wine of trembling.

4 You have given a banner to those who revere You,
   to let them flee out of the range of bow.

5 Save them by Your right hand and answer me,
that Your beloved may be delivered.
6 God has spoken from the Sanctuary:
"With delight, I will divide up Shechem,
and apportion out the Vale of Succoth.

7 Mine is Gilead, mine is Manasseh;
Ephraim is the strength of My crown,
Judah my commander's baton.

8 Moab is my washbasin,
upon Edom I will plant my sandals,
over Philistia I will shout in triumph."

9 Who will bring me to the fortified city?
Who will lead me to Edom?
10 Have not You, O God, rejected us?
Will You not march, O God, with our armies?

11 Grant us deliverance from our foes,
for worthless is human help!
12 With You, O God, we shall do mighty deeds,
for it is You Who trample down our foes.

PSALM 61
Prayer of an Exile for Protection

To the choir director: with stringed instruments.
A Psalm of David.

1 Hear my cry, O God,
listen to my prayer!
2 From the brink of the nether world
I cry to You, as my heart grows faint.
O set me high upon the Rock,
and there give me rest.

3 For You are my refuge,
a tower of strength against my enemy.

4 Let me dwell in Your shelter for ever!
   safe under the shelter of Your wings!

5 O that You would accept my vows, O God,
   and would grant me the heritage
   of those who revere Your Name.

6 May You lengthen the life of the ruler,
   and whose reign may continue age after age.
7 May the ruler be enthroned before God for ever,
   and appoint faithful love and constancy as guards.

8 So will I ever sing praises to Your Name,
   fulfilling my vows day after day.

PSALM 62
Confident Prayer of Trust in God

To the choir director: "al Jeduthun."
A Psalm of David.

1 In God alone there is rest, my soul,
   from Whom comes my deliverance.
2 God alone is my Rock, and my deliverance,
   and my fortress where I stand unshaken.

3 How long will you threaten a person
   all together, intent on murder;
   you shall be like a crumbling wall
   and as a tottering fence.

4 They plotted to cast their victim down
   from the coveted place of honor.
   They delight in their deceptions.
   They pronounce a blessing with their mouths,
   but they curse in their heart.

5 In God alone there is rest, my soul,
   Who truly is the source of my hope.

6 God alone is my Rock, and my deliverance,
   and my fortress where I stand unshaken.

7 With God rests my deliverance and my glory;
   my mighty Rock, my refuge is God.

8 Trust in God at all times, you people;
   pour out your heart before Yahweh;
   God is a refuge for us.

9 Those of low estate are but a breath,
   those of high estate are a delusion;
   on scales they are lighter than leaves,
   they are together lighter than a breath.

10 Put no trust in extortion,
   no empty hopes in robbery;
   however much wealth may multiply,
   do not set your heart on it.

11 God has spoken once,
   twice have I heard this:
   that power belongs to God,

12 to You, Adonai, faithful love;
   and You reward all according to their deeds.

PSALM 63
Ardent Longing for God

A Psalm of David, when he was in the Wilderness of Judah.

1 God, You are my God, I pine for You,
   my soul thirsts for You;
   my body longs for You,
   more than parched and weary land for water.

2 Thus I have gazed on You in the sanctuary,
   beholding Your power and glory.

3 For Your faithful love is better than life,
   my lips will give praise to You.

4 Thus I will bless You all my life,
   in Your Name I will lift up my hands.
5 My soul will be enriched as with a rich feast
   and my mouth will praise You with joyful lips.

6 When I remember You upon my bed,
   I will ponder on You in the watches of the night.
7 For You have always been my Helper,
   and in the shadow of Your wings I sing for joy.
8 My soul clings to You;
   Your right hand upholds me.

9 May those who seek to destroy my life
   go down into the depths of the earth.
10 May they fall to the power of the sword,
   may they be left as prey for jackals.
11 Then the ruler shall rejoice in God;
   all who swear by You shall glory;
   for the mouths of liars shall be silenced.

PSALM 64
Prayer for Deliverance from Enemies

To the choir director.
A Psalm of David.

1 Listen to my voice, O God, as I pray,
   protect my life from fear of the enemy.
2 Hide me from the secret plots of the wicked,
   from the wrath of the evildoers.

3 They sharpen their tongues like swords,
   and aim poisonous abuse like arrows.
4 They shoot from ambush at the virtuous,
   they shoot suddenly and without fear.

5 They support each other in their evil plans
   they discuss how to lay their snares,
   'Who will see us?' they say.

6 They search into injustice, thinking,
   'We have finished a well-laid plan.'
   Who can penetrate human nature
   in its inward mind and the depths of the heart?

7 But God will shoot an arrow at them;
   and their wounds shall suddenly appear.
8 So shall their tongue be silenced;
   all who see them will shake their heads.

9 Then everyone will be awestruck
   they will proclaim what God has done,
   and in wisdom consider what God has done.

10 Let the just rejoice in Yahweh,
    and take refuge in God!
    Let all the just in heart glory!

PSALM 65
A Hymn of Public Thanksgiving

To the choir director.
A Psalm of David. A Song.

1 Praise is befitting You,
   O God, in Zion;
   and to You shall vows be fulfilled.

2 To You Who hear our prayers,
   all flesh shall come.
3 Our wicked deeds are beyond number,
   our rebellious deeds, but You wipe them out.

4 How blessed are those whom You choose
   and invite to dwell in Your courts!
   We shall be satisfied with the goodness
   of Your house, Your holy temple!

5 You answer us, O God, our Savior
   with the marvels of your saving justice.

You are the hope of all the ends of the earth,
and of the sea, of those afar off.

6 By Your strength the mountains are set,
banded together with might.

7 You silence the roaring of the seas,
the roaring of their waves,
and the turmoil of the peoples.

8 Those who live to the ends of the earth
shall tremble at Your wonders;
for Your miracles bring shouts of joy,
to the gateways of morning and evening.

9 You visit the earth and water it,
You make it fruitful with your rain;
the river of God brims over with water;
in this way You prepare the earth,
and provide Your people with grain.

10 You fill earth's terraces with water;
You deepen its furrows;
You make it soft with showers,
and You bless its sproutings.

11 You crown the year with Your bounty,
and the pastures drip with fatness.

12 The pastures of the wilderness drip,
the hills gird themselves with joy.

13 The meadows clothe themselves with flocks,
the valleys deck themselves with wheat,
they shall rejoice, yea, they shall sing.

PSALM 66
Communal Prayer of Thanksgiving

To the choir director. A Song. A Psalm.

1 Make a joyful noise to God,
  all the earth!
2 Sing to God for God's Glorious Name;
  give to God glorious praise!

3 Say to God, "How awesome are Your deeds!
  So great is Your power
  that Your enemies prostrate before You.
4 All the earth bows down before You;
  they sing praises to You,
  sing praises to Your Name."

5 Come and see the marvels of God,
  Whose deeds are awesome among the people.
6 God turned the sea into dry land;
  they passed through the river on foot.
  Come let us rejoice in God,

7 Who rules with might for ever,
  Whose eyes keep watch on the nations,
  let not the rebellious exalt themselves.

8 Bless our God, O peoples,
  with loud voice proclaim God's praises,
9 Who has kept us among the living,
  and keeps our feet from stumbling.

10 For You, O God, have tested us;
  You have refined us as silver is refined.
11 You have brought us into the snare,
  You have laid heavy burdens on our backs.

12 You have caused us to be in servitude;
  we went through fire and through water;
  but finally You brought us to the land of plenty.

13 I will bring burnt offerings into Your house,
    I will fulfill my vows to You,
14 the vows which my lips uttered
    and my mouth promised when I was in trouble.

15 I will offer You burnt offerings of fatlings,
    together with the smoke of the burning rams;
    I will sacrifice to You bullocks and goats.

16 Come and listen, all who revere God,
    and I will tell what God has done for me.
17 To God I cried aloud
    high praise was on my tongue.

18 If I were conscious of wickedness in my heart,
    Adonai, would not have heard me.
19 But, in fact God did hear me
    and heeded my voice in prayer.

20 Blessed be God,
    Who has not turned away my prayer
    Whose faithful love is not withdrawn from me.

PSALM 67
Thanksgiving Harvest Song

To the choir director: with stringed instruments.
A Psalm. A Song.

1 God, be gracious to us and bless us
   and make Your face to shine upon us,
2 that Your ways may be known upon earth,
   Your saving power among all nations.

3 Let the peoples thank You, O God;
   let all the peoples thank You!

4 Let the nations be glad and sing for joy,
   for You judge the peoples with justice
   and govern the nations on earth.

5   Let the peoples thank You, O God;
    let all the peoples thank You!

6   May the earth yield its produce,
    may God, our God, bless us.

7   May God continue to bless us;
    and be revered to the ends of the earth.

PSALM 68
Hymn to the Most High of Israel

To the choir director. A Psalm of David. A Song.

1   O God, arise and scatter Your enemies;
    let Your opponents flee before You.

2   You disperse them like smoke;
    as wax melts in the presence of fire,
    so the wicked perish in Your presence!

3   But let the just be joyful;
    let them exult in Your presence;
    let them be jubilant with joy!

4   We sing to You God,
    we sing praises to Your Name.
    We extol You Who ride upon the clouds;
    Your Name is Yahweh, we exult before You!

5   God, in Your holy dwelling
    You give a loving home to orphans
    and justice to widows.

6   God, You give the desolate a home to live in;
    You lead out the prisoners to prosperity;
    but make the rebellious dwell in a parched land.

7   O God, when You went out before Your people,
    when You marched through the wilderness,

8   the earth quaked, at the presence of God,
    the heavens poured down rain;

   even Sinai quaked at the presence of God,
   the God of Israel.

9   God, You rained down a shower of blessings,
    You restored Your heritage as it languished.
10 Your family found a home, which You,
    in Your goodness provided for the needy.

11 Adonai gave a command,
    good tidings of a countless army.
12 The rulers of armies fled, they ran away!
    Those that stayed at home divided the spoil.

13 When You stay among the sheepfolds,
    the wings of a dove are covered with silver,
    and their feathers with gleaming gold.
14 When Shaddai scattered rulers in it,
    snow fell on Mount Salmon.

15 The mountain of Bashan is God's mountain,
    mountain of Bashan is a mountain of peaks.
16 Why be envious, O mountain ranges,
    at the mount which God has chosen for an abode,
    where Yahweh will dwell for ever?

17 The chariots of God are thousand upon thousand,
    Adonai has come from Sinai to the holy place.
18 When You ascended on high,
    You lead captives in Your train,
    You received gifts from all, even from rebels,
    that Yahweh God may have a dwelling-place.

19 Blessed are You, Adonai, day after day,
    You carry our burdens, O God our Savior.

20 Our God is a God of deliverance;
    from Adonai God comes escape from death.
21 God, You shatter the head of Your enemies,
    the long-haired skull of the prowling criminal.

22 Adonai said, "I will bring them back from Bashan,
   I will bring them back from the depths of the sea,
23 that you may bathe your feet in blood,
   and the tongues of your dogs may feast on your foes."

24 Your processions, O God, are for all to see
   the processions of my Sovereign God, to the sanctuary;
25 the singers went in front, the musicians last,
   in the middle were maidens playing the timbrels.

26 "O Bless God in the great assembly,
   Adonai, You are the fountain of Israel."
27 There was little Benjamin in their front,
   the leaders of Judah in their throng,
   the leaders of Zebulun and the leaders of Naphtali.

28 Summon Your might, O God;
   show Your strength, O God,
   which You have wielded for us.
29 Because of Your temple at Jerusalem
   rulers will bring gifts to You.

30 Rebuke the wild beasts of the reeds,
   that herd of bulls, that people of calves,
   those idols that are covered with silver.
   Scatter the peoples who delight in war.
31 Ambassadors shall come from Egypt;
   Ethiopia shall stretch out hands to God.

32 Sing to God, O dominions of the earth;
   O sing praises unto Adonai,
33 Who ride in the heavens, the ancient heavens,
   to the One Who sends out the word, a mighty word.

34 Ascribe strength to God over Israel,
   God's majesty and strength in the skies.
35 O God You are Awesome in Your sanctuary,
   You are the God of Israel,
   the One Who gives strength and power to the people.
   Blessed be God!

PSALM 69
Prayer for Deliverance from Death

To the choir director: to the tune of "Lilies."
A Psalm of David.

1　Save me, O God!
　　For the waters have come to engulf me.
2　I sink in deep mire
　　where there is no footing;
　　I have come into deep waters,
　　where floods sweep over me.
3　I am exhausted with my crying;
　　my throat is withered.
　　My eyes are worn out,
　　with searching for my God.

4　They that hate me without a cause,
　　are more than the hairs of my head.
　　Mighty are those who seek to destroy me
　　those that attack me with their lies.
　　(Must I now return what I did not steal?)
5　O God, You know how foolish I am;
　　my sinfulness is not hidden from You.

6　Let not those who trust in You be put to shame
　　Adonai, Yahweh Sabaoth, because of me;
　　let not those who seek You be disgraced,
　　O God of Israel, because of me.
7　It is for You I bear insults,
　　my face is covered with shame.
8　I have become a stranger to my kindred,
　　an alien to my own mother's children.

9　For zeal for Your house has consumed me,
　　the insults directed against You have fallen on me.
10　When I mortified my soul with fasting,
　　I found myself insulted for it.

11 When I made sackcloth my clothing,
    I became a mockery to them.
12 They who sit at the gate gossiped about me,
    and the inebriated made songs about me.

13 And so this is my prayer to You, O Yahweh,
    at the time of Your favor, O God,
    in the abundance of Your faithful love, answer me,
    in the constancy of Your saving power.

14 Rescue me from the mire before I sink in,
    deliver me from those who hate me,
    and out of the waters that are deep.
15 Let not the waves wash over me,
    nor the deep swallow me up,
    nor the pit close its mouth over me.

16 Listen to me, O Yahweh,
    for Your faithful love is compassionate;
    in Your great compassion, turn towards me.
17 Hide not Your face from Your servant;
    make haste to answer me, for I am in distress.
18 Draw near to me, redeem me,
    ransom me because of my enemies!

19 You know well the insults,
    the shame and the disgrace I endure.
    Every one of my foes is known to You.
20 Insults have broken my heart, I am sick,
    I waited for one to show pity, but there was none;
    and for consolers, but I found no one.

21 They gave me bitter herbs for my food,
    and in my thirst they gave me vinegar to drink.
22 Let their own table become a trap before them;
    let their abundance be a snare.
23 Let their eyes grow so dim, that they see not;
    and all their muscles lose their strength.

24 Pour out Your indignation upon them,
    and let Your burning anger overtake them.
25 May their home be a desolation,
    let no one dwell in their tents.
26 For they persecuted the one already stricken,
    and afflicted more the one already wounded.

27 Charge them with crime after crime;
    may they never receive Your saving justice.
28 Blot them out from the Book of Life
    let them not be enrolled among the just.

29 But I am afflicted and in pain;
    let Your deliverance, O God, set me on high!
30 I will praise the Name of God with a song;
    I will magnify God with thanksgiving.
31 This will please Yahweh more than bulls
    horned or hoofed bulls.

32 Let the oppressed see it and be glad;
    you who seek God, let your hearts revive.
33 For Yahweh listens to the poor,
    and does not despise those in prisons.
34 Let heaven and earth praise Yahweh,
    the seas and everything that moves in them.

35 For God will save Zion
    and rebuild the cities of Judah;
    and they shall live there and possess it.
36 The descendants of Your servants shall inherit it,
    and those who love Your Name shall dwell in it.

PSALM 70
A Prayer for Divine Assistance

To the choir director.
A Psalm of David, for the memorial offering.

1 Be pleased, O God, to rescue me,
   O Yahweh, make haste to help me!

2   Let those who seek my life be ashamed,
    let them be confounded.
    Let them be turned backward and shamed,
    those who delight in my misfortunes.
3   Let them shrink away covered with shame
    all those who say to me, "Aha, Aha!"

4   May all who seek You rejoice
    and be glad in You!
    May those who love Your saving justice
    say evermore, "God is great!"

5   But I am poor and needy;
    come quickly to me, O God!
    You are my help and my deliverer.
    O Yahweh, do not wait any longer.

PSALM 71
A Prayer in Old Age

1   In You, O Yahweh, I take refuge;
    let me never be put to shame!
2   In Your justice deliver me and rescue me;
    incline Your ear to me, and save me!

3   Be a Rock of strength for me,
    a strong fortress, to save me,
    for You are my Rock and my fortress.
4   My God, rescue me from the clutches of the wicked,
    from the grasp of the ruthless and the unjust.

5   For You, O Yahweh, are my hope,
    my trust, O Adonai, from my youth.
6   It was You Who sustained me from my birth;
    it was You Who took me from my mother's womb.
    Constant has been my hope in You.

7   I am like a wonder to many;
    but You are my strong refuge.

8 My mouth is filled with Your praise,
and with Your glory all day long.

9 Do not cast me off in the time of old age;
forsake me not when my strength fails.

10 For my enemies speak against me,
those who watch for my life counsel together.

11 They say to me, "God has forsaken you;
we will pursue and seize you,
for there is none to rescue you."

12 O God, be not far from me;
O my God, make haste to help me!

13 Let them be ashamed,
let the enemies of my soul be consumed,
let them be covered with disgrace,
let those seeking evil for me be dishonored.

14 As for me, I will pray continually,
and will praise You yet more and more.

15 My mouth will proclaim Your justice,
all day long Your deeds of saving justice,
for their number is past my knowledge.

16 I will come in the strength of Yahweh,
I will praise Your justice, Yours alone.

17 O God, from my youth You have taught me,
and I still proclaim Your wondrous deeds.

18 And now that I am old and gray-haired,
O God, forsake me not,
till I proclaim Your strength to all ages,
Your power to everyone who is to come.

19 Your justice, O God, reaches the high heavens.
You Who have done great things,
O God, who is like You?

20 You Who have shown me much misery and hardship,
shall turn to me and revive me again;

You will turn from the depths of the earth,
and will bring me up again.
21 You will increase my honor,
and surround and comfort me again.

22 I will also praise You with the harp
for Your faithfulness, O my God;
I will sing praises to You with the lyre,
O Holy One of Israel.

23 My lips shall shout for joy,
when I sing praises to You;
my soul also, which You have rescued.
24 And my tongue shall muse on Your justice
all day long,
for those seeking my harm are disgraced,
they are put to shame.

PSALM 72
A Prayer for a Royal Ruler

A Psalm of Solomon.

1 "God, endow Your ruler with Your judgment
and with Your justice, the royal offspring!"
2 May you, (O ruler), judge God's people with justice,
and the oppressed with fairness!

3 May the mountains bring peace to your people,
and the hills your justice!
4 May you defend the oppressed of the people,
give freedom to the children of the needy,
and crush their oppressors!

5 May you endure as long as the sun and the moon,
through all generations!
6 May you be like rainfall on the mown grass,
like showers upon the scorched land!

7   May justice flourish in your days,
    and peace abound, till the moon be no more!
8   May your dominion stretch from sea to sea,
    from the river to the ends of the earth!

9   May the desert tribes bow down before you,
    and all your enemies lick the dust!
10 May the rulers of Tarshish and the islands
    render you tribute,
    and may the rulers of Sheba and Seba
    bring you gifts!
11 May all rulers bow down before you,
    and all nations serve you!

12 May you rescue the needy crying for help,
    and the oppressed who have no helper.
13 May you have pity on the poor and the needy,
    and save the lives of the needy.

14 May you redeem their lives from tyranny and force,
    their blood is precious in your sight.
15 May you have long life
    receiving gold from Sheba as a gift!
    May prayers be offered for you constantly
    and blessings invoked throughout the day!

16 May wheat abound in the land,
    waving on the peak of the mountains.
    May its fruits dance like Lebanon;
    may people flourish in the cities,
    like the grass of the field!

17 May your name be blessed for ever,
    and your fame continue as long as the sun;
    bringing a blessing on all races of the world,
    and blessed in turn by all the nations.

18 "Blessed are You Yahweh, the God of Israel,
    Who alone work marvelous deeds.

19 Blessed be Your glorious Name for ever;
    may the whole earth be filled with Your glory!
    Amen and Amen!''

20 End of the prayers of David, son of Jesse.

BOOK THREE
Psalms 73-89

PSALM 73
A Reflection on the Justice of God

A Psalm of Asaph.

1 Truly God is good, O Israel,
   to those who are pure of heart.

2 My feet had almost stumbled,
   my steps had well nigh slipped.
3 For I was envious of the arrogant,
   I saw the prosperity of the wicked.

4 For them there are no struggles,
   their body is sound and sleek.
5 They are not in trouble like other mortals;
   they are not stricken like other people.

6 They wear pride as their necklace;
   injustice covers them like a garment.
7 Their eyes swell out with fatness,
   the fancies of their hearts exceed all bounds.

8 They imagine and speak with malice;
   they talk unjustly against the Most High.

9   They set their mouths against the heavens,
    and their tongue walks through the earth.

10 Therefore the people turn and praise them;
    and drink up their words in abundance.

11 And they say, "How can God know?
    Does the Most High ever take notice?"

12 Look at them, such are the wicked;
    always carefree, they increase riches.

13 How useless, that I kept my heart pure,
    and washed my hands in innocence

14 For all the day long I have been stricken,
    and have been disciplined every morning.

15 If I had said, "I shall talk like them,"
    I would have betrayed Your children's race.

16 But when I tried to understand this,
    it was too painful in my eyes;

17 until I went into the sanctuary of God,
    then I understood what was to become of them.

18 Surely You set them on a slippery slope;
    You make them slide to collapse.

19 How they became desolation in an instant,
    swept away, consumed utterly with terrors!

20 They are like a dream upon waking, Adonai,
    on awaking, You dismiss their image.

21 My heart grew embittered,
    and I was pierced in my reins.

22 I was a stupid fool without understanding,
    was like a mere beast in Your presence.

23 Even so I stayed in Your presence
    You grasped me by Your right hand.

24 You guide me with Your counsel,
    and then take me to Your glory.

25 Whom have I in heaven but You?
    And with You, I lack nothing on earth.
26 My flesh and my heart waste away,
    but God is the rock of my heart
    and my portion for ever.

27 Those who go far from You shall perish;
    You destroy those who are false to You.
28 As for me, it is good to be near God;
    I have made Adonai Yahweh my refuge,
    that I may proclaim all Your works.

PSALM 74
National Mourning and Plea for Relief

A Maskil—An Instruction of Asaph.

1 God, why have You rejected us for ever?
   Your anger blazing against the sheep of Your pasture?
2 Remember the people You took to Yourself long ago,
   Your own tribe which You redeemed;
   Remember Mount Zion, where You have dwelt.

3 Direct Your steps to the perpetual ruins;
   the enemy have sacked everything in the sanctuary!
4 Your opponents made uproar in the place of assemblies,
   they set up their own emblems by the hundreds.

5 They set fire to the upper entrance,
   while axes hacked at the paneling.
6 They cut down all its carved wood
   they battered with hatchets and hammers.
7 They set Your sanctuary on fire;
   they utterly desecrated Your Name's abode.

8 They said in their hearts,
   "Let us crush them at one stroke,
   burn down all sacred shrines in the land."

9   We see no signs, no prophet any more,
    and none of us knows how long it will last.

10 O God, how long shall the enemy blaspheme?
    Shall the enemy malign Your Name for ever?

11 Why do You withdraw Your hand,
    why do You keep Your right hand in Your bosom?

12 For God is my Sovereign from of old,
    working deliverance in the midst of the earth.

13 You broke the sea by Your strength;
    You burst the heads of the monsters on the waters.

14 You cracked open the heads of Leviathan,
    You gave it as food to the wild animals.

15 You released the springs and brooks;
    You dried up ever-flowing rivers.

16 Yours is the day, Yours also the night;
    You established the luminaries and the sun.

17 You fixed all the boundaries of the earth;
    You created summer and winter.

18 Remember, O Yahweh, the enemy's blasphemy,
    an impious people defames Your Name.

19 Do not surrender Your turtledove to the beast;
    do not forget the life of Your poor for ever.

20 Look to Your covenant;
    all the hiding-places of the land are full,
    the abodes of violence.

21 Let not the downtrodden be put to shame;
    let the poor and needy praise Your Name.

22 Arise, O God, prosecute Your cause;
    remember how the fools blaspheme You all day long.

23 Do not forget the clamor of Your enemies,
    the ever-mounting uproar of Your adversaries.

PSALM 75
Thanksgiving for God's Just Governance

To the choir director: to the tune of "Do Not Destroy."
A Psalm of Asaph. A Song.

1 We give You thanks, O God,
  we give You thanks.
  We call on Your Name,
  we recount Your wonderful works.

2 At the appointed time,
  I myself shall dispense justice.
3 When the earth quakes, and all its inhabitants,
  it is I who keep steady its pillars.

4 I said to the boastful, "Do not boast,"
  and to the wicked, "Do not lift up your horn;
5 do not lift up your horn on high,
  or speak with that irreverent stance."

6 For exaltations are not from the east
  nor from the west nor from the desert;
7 but it is God Who executes judgment,
  putting down one and lifting up another.

8 Yahweh is holding a cup in hand,
  filled with a heady blend of foaming wine.
  Yahweh will pour it, and they will drink it,
  all the wicked on earth will drink it to the dregs.

9 But I will rejoice for ever,
  I will sing praises to the God of Jacob.
10 All the horns of the wicked will be cut off,
  but the horns of the just shall be exalted.

PSALM 76
Hymn to Awesome God

To the choir director: with stringed instruments.
A Psalm of Asaph. A Song.

1 God, You are acknowledged in Judah
Your Name is great in Israel.

2 Your tent has been pitched in Salem,
Your dwelling place in Zion.

3 There You broke the flashing arrows,
the shield, the sword, and the weapons of war.

4 Glorious are You,
more majestic than the mountains of prey.

5 The stouthearted have been stripped;
they slept their last sleep;
the warriors' arms have failed them.

6 At Your rebuke, O God of Jacob,
both rider and horse stand stunned.

7 But You, Awesome are You!
When You are angry who can stand before You?

8 From heaven Your verdicts thunder,
the earth is still with dread,

9 when God takes stand to give judgment
to save all the oppressed of the earth.

10 Human wrath serves only to praise You;
the survivors of Your rage will encircle You.

11 Make and fulfill your vows to Yahweh your God;
let all who are around
bring gifts to the Awesome One,

12 Who cuts short the breath of the noble ones,
Who is awesome to the rulers of the earth.

PSALM 77
Israel's Past: A Meditation

To the choir director: "al Jeduthun."
A Psalm of Asaph.

1   I cry to God in my distress,
    I cry to God Who listens to me.

2   In the day of my distress I sought Adonai;
    all night I tirelessly stretched out my hands;
    my soul refused to be comforted.

3   I sigh as I think of God,
    my spirit faints away as I meditate.

4   You kept my eyelids from closing;
    I am in distress that I cannot speak.

5   I considered the days of old,
    years long past I recalled.

6   I meditated far into the night
    I communed with my own heart;
    I have examined my soul and said:

7   "Will You abandon us, Adonai, for ever,
    and never again be favorable?

8   Has Your faithful love for ever ceased?
    Has Your word for all time come to an end?

9   Have You forgotten to be gracious, O God?
    Will You in anger shut off Your tender mercies?"

10 And I said, "This is my infirmity,
    a visitation of the power of the Most High."

11 I will call to mind the deeds of Yahweh;
    yes, I will remember Your wonders of old.

12 I will meditate on all Your works,
    and ponder on Your mighty deeds.

13 Your way, O God, is holy.
    What god is great like our God?

14 You are the God who works wonders,
Who manifest Your might among the peoples.
15 Who with Your own arm redeemed Your people,
the children of Jacob and Joseph.

16 When the waters saw You, O God,
when the waters saw You,
they writhed in anguish
yes, the very depths shook with fear.
17 The clouds poured out water;
the skies gave forth thunder;
Your arrows flashed on every side.

18 The crash of Your thunder was heard;
Your lightning lit up the world;
the earth trembled and shook.
19 Your way is in the sea,
Your path is in the great waters;
yet none could trace Your footprints.

20 You guided Your people like a flock
by the hand of Moses and Aaron.

PSALM 78
God's Goodness and Israel's Ingratitude

A Maskil—An Instruction of Asaph.

1 "Give ear, O my people, to my teaching;
incline your ears to the words of my mouth!
2 I will open my mouth in a parable;
I will utter proverbs of old.

3 That which we have heard and known,
and which our ancestors have told us.
4 We shall not conceal from their descendants,
but will tell to a generation still to come;
the glorious deeds and power of Yahweh,
and the wonders which God has done."

5 O God, You instituted a witness in Jacob,
and established a law in Israel,
You commanded our ancestors
to hand it down to their descendants;

6 that the generation to come might know it,
the children yet to be born.
They should tell to their own children,
7 that they set their hope in You, O God,
never forgetting Your great deeds,
but always observing Your commandments.

8 They were not to be like their ancestors,
a stubborn and rebellious generation,
a generation whose heart was not firm,
whose spirit was unfaithful to You, God.

9 The Ephraimites, armed with the bow,
turned back on the day of battle.
10 They did not keep Your covenant, O God,
but refused to walk according to Your law.

11 They had forgotten Your great deeds,
and the marvels You had shown them,
12 the marvels You did before their ancestors
in the land of Egypt, in the fields of Zoan.

13 You divided the sea and led them through,
and caused the waters to stand like a dike.
14 You led them by a cloud in the day,
and through the night by light of fire.

15 You split the rocks in the wilderness,
and let them drink as from a great well.
16 You brought forth streams out of the rock,
and caused waters to run down like torrents.

17 Yet they continued to sin against God
defying the Most High in the desert.

18 They deliberately challenged God
by demanding the food they craved.

19 They spoke against God saying,
"Can God spread a table in the desert?
20 True when God struck the rock
water gushed out and streams overflowed.
Can God also give bread,
or provide meat for this people?"

21 When You, O Yahweh, heard them
You vented your anger,
Your fire blazed against Jacob,
Your anger mounted against Israel;
22 because they had no faith in You,
and did not trust in Your saving power.

23 Yet You commanded the skies above,
and opened the doors of heaven;
24 and You rained down manna to feed them,
and gave them grain of heaven.
25 Mere mortals ate of the bread of the Mighty;
You sent them provisions in abundance.

26 You roused an east wind from heaven,
and by Your power dispatched the south wind;
27 You rained on them meat like dust,
birds thick as the sand of the seas;
28 You let them fall amidst their camp,
all around their habitations.

29 And they ate and were well filled,
for You gave them what they craved.
30 But their cravings were still upon them,
while the food was still in their mouths,
31 Your anger, O God, rose against them
and You slew the strongest of them,
You struck down the choice ones of Israel.

32 In spite of all this, they still sinned;
despite Your wonders they did not believe.
33 So You made their days vanish like a breath,
and their years in sudden terror.

34 When You slew them, they sought for You;
they repented and sought You earnestly.
35 They remembered that God was their rock,
God the Most High their redeemer.

36 But they flattered You with their mouths;
with their tongues they lied to You.
37 Their hearts were not loyal to You;
they were not faithful to Your covenant.

38 Yet You the Merciful forgave their sin,
and did not destroy them.
Time and again You restrained Your anger,
and held back the stirrings of Your wrath.
39 You remembered that they were mere mortals,
a passing breath that never returns.

40 How often they defied You in the wilderness
and grieved You in the wastelands!
41 They challenged God again and again,
provoking the Holy One of Israel.

42 They did not remember Your power,
the day You saved them from their oppressor,
43 when You wrought Your signs in Egypt,
and Your miracles in the fields of Zoan.

44 You turned their rivers and streams to blood,
that they had nothing to drink.
45 You sent swarms of flies to devour them,
and frogs to devastate them.

46 You consigned their crops to the grasshoppers,
and the fruit of their labor to the locust.

47 You destroyed their vines with hail,
and their sycamore trees with frost.

48 You gave over their cattle to the hail,
and their flocks to thunderbolts.

49 You let loose on them Your blazing anger,
fury, rage and destruction,
a battalion of destroying angels.

50 You made a path for Your anger;
You did not spare them from death,
but gave their lives over to the plague.

51 You struck all the first-born in Egypt,
the first-fruits of strength in the tents of Ham.

52 You led forth Your people like sheep,
guiding them in the wasteland like a flock.

53 You guided them securely and unafraid;
while the sea engulfed their enemies.

54 You brought them to Your holy mount,
the hill-country Your right hand had won.

55 You dispossessed nations before them;
You apportioned them for a possession
settling the tribes of Israel in their tents.

56 Still they challenged You, the Most High God,
and defied You refusing to keep Your decrees.

57 Perverse and treacherous like their ancestors,
they were twisted like a deceitful bow.

58 They enraged You with their high places,
and provoked Your jealousy with their idols.

59 You listened and were full of wrath,
You utterly rejected Israel.

60 You abandoned Your dwelling in Shiloh,
the tent You pitched among mortals.

61 You delivered Your strength to captivity,
Your glorious ark into the hand of the foe.

62 You handed over Your people to the sword,
    and vented Your wrath on Your heritage.
63 Fire devoured their young men,
    their young girls had no wedding-song.

64 Their priests fell by the sword,
    and their widows sang no dirges.
65 Then You awoke, Adonai, as one asleep
    like a champion overcome with wine.

66 You caused Your adversaries to retreat;
    You put them to an everlasting shame.
67 Rejecting the tents of Joseph,
    and passing over the tribe of Ephraim,

68 You chose the tribe of Judah,
    Your well-beloved Mount Zion.
69 You built Your sanctuary like high places,
    like the earth set firm for ever.

70 You chose David to be Your servant,
    took him from the sheepfold;
71 took him from tending the sheep,
    to pasture Jacob your people,
    and Israel Your inheritance.
72 With blameless heart David tended them,
    and guided them with skillful hands.

PSALM 79
A Lament over the Destruction of Jerusalem

A Psalm of Asaph.

 1 O God, the nations have invaded Your heritage;
    they have defiled Your holy temple;
    they have laid Jerusalem in ruins.
 2 They have left the corpses of Your servants
    as food for the birds of the air
    the bodies of Your faithful for the wild beasts.

3   They shed blood like water all around Jerusalem
    leaving no one to bury them.
4   We have become a scorn to our neighbors,
    mockery and derision to those all around us.
5   How long will You be angry, O Yahweh? for ever?
    How long will Your jealous wrath burn like fire?
6   Pour out Your anger on the nations
    who do not acknowledge You,
    and on the peoples who do not call on Your Name!
7   For they have devoured the house of Jacob,
    and laid waste their dwelling-place.

8   Do not impute to us our ancestors' sins;
    in Your compassion swiftly come to meet us,
    for we are utterly weakened.
9   Help us, O God of our deliverance,
    rescue us, for the glory of Your Name,
    forgive our sins, for Your Name's sake!

10 Why should the nations ask, "Where is their God?"
    Make Yourself known among the nations
    by avenging the outpoured blood of Your servants.
11 May the groans of the prisoners reach You;
    by Your great power rescue those doomed to die!

12 Repay our neighbors sevenfold, O Adonai,
    for the insults they have leveled at You.
13 Then we, Your people, the flock of Your pasture,
    will give You thanks for ever;
    we will recount Your praises from age to age.

PSALM 80
Prayer for the Restoration of Israel

To the choir director: to the tune of "Lilies."
A Testimony of Asaph. A Psalm.

1   Listen, O Shepherd of Israel,
    You Who lead Joseph like a flock!
    Shine forth, You Who dwell among the cherubs.

2   Before Ephraim and Benjamin and Manasseh
     show forth Your power and come to save us!

3   Bring us back, O God Sabaoth;
     let Your face shine on us, and we shall be safe.

4   O God, Yahweh Sabaoth, how long?
     How long will You be deaf to Your people's prayers?
5   You have made them eat the bread of tears,
     and given them tears to drink in full measure.
6   You have made us a mockery for our neighbors;
     and our enemies laugh among themselves.

7   Bring us back, O God Sabaoth;
     let Your face shine on us, and we shall be safe.

8   You brought a vine from Egypt;
     You drove out the nations and planted it.
9   You cleared the ground for it;
     it took root and filled the whole land.

10 The mountains were covered with its shade,
     its boughs were like the robust cedars;
11 its branches stretched as far as the sea,
     its shoots as far as the River.

12 Why then have You broken down its fences,
     that the passers-by pluck its fruit?
13 The boars from the forest ravage it,
     and beasts of the field feed on it.

14 Come back to us, O God Sabaoth!
     Look down from heaven,
     see and visit this vine,
15 and the vineyard which Your right hand planted,
     and the branch You made strong for Yourself.
16 They cut it down and burned it with fire;
     may they perish before You at Your rebuke!

17 May Your hand protect those at Your right hand,
     those You made strong for Yourself!

18 Never again will we turn away from You;
    give us life, and we will call on Your Name!

19 Bring us back, O God Sabaoth;
    let Your face shine on us, and we shall be safe.

PSALM 81
Joyful Hymn to God, the Lawgiver

To the choir director: on an instrument of Gath.
A Psalm of Asaph.

1 Sing aloud to God, our strength;
   shout for joy to the God of Jacob!

2 Sing a psalm, sound the tambourine,
   the pleasant lyre with the psaltery.
3 Blow the trumpet for the new moon,
   at the full moon, on our feast day.

4 For it is a statute, O Israel,
   an ordinance of the God of Jacob,
5 a decree imposed on Joseph,
   when he went out to the land of Egypt,
   I heard the voice of the one unknown to me:

6 "I removed the yoke from your shoulder,
   I released your hands from the bonds.
7 In distress you called, and I delivered you,
   I sheltered you under my glorious cover,
   I tested you at the waters of Meribah.

8 Listen, O my people, while I admonish you!
   O Israel, if only you would listen to me!
9 There shall be no alien god among you;
   you shall not bow down to a strange god.

10 I, Yahweh, am your God,
   Who brought you up out of the land of Egypt.
   Open your mouth wide, and I will fill it.

11 But my people would not listen to me;
    Israel would have none of me.
12 So I left them to their own defiant ways,
    to follow their own devices.

13 O that my people would listen to me,
    that Israel would walk in my ways!
14 I would soon have subdued their enemies,
    and turned my hand against their enemies.

15 Those who hate Yahweh have lied to me,
    but they shall tremble for ever.
16 I would feed you with the finest of wheat,
    and with honey from the rock I would satisfy you."

PSALM 82
Prayer the Restoration of Universal Peace
A Psalm of Asaph.

1 God presides in the divine council;
   God judges in the midst of the gods:
2 "How much longer will you judge unjustly
   and lift up the faces of the wicked?

3 Vindicate the poor and the orphan;
   do justice to the afflicted and the needy.
4 Rescue the poor and the needy;
   save them from the hand of the wicked."

5 They do not know, and do not understand,
   they walk about in darkness;
   all the foundations of the earth are shaken.

6 I had thought, "You are gods,
   children of the Most High, all of you;
7 nevertheless, you shall die like mortals,
   and fall like one of the rulers."

8 Arise, O God, judge the earth;
   for all nations belong to You!

PSALM 83
Prayer on Behalf of the Nation
for Deliverance

A Song. A Psalm of Asaph.

1 O God, do not remain silent;
   be not quiet, O God, and be not still!
2 See how Your enemies are in turmoil;
   how Your foes lift up their heads.

3 They lay crafty plans against Your people;
   they conspire against Your chosen ones.
4 They say, "Come, let us wipe them out as a nation;
   let the name 'Israel' be remembered no more!"

5 Yes, they conspire with a single mind;
   they conclude an alliance against You—
6 the tents of Edom and the Ishmaelites,
   Moab and the Hagrites,

7 Gebal and Ammon and Amalek,
   Philistia and the inhabitants of Tyre.
8 Even Assyria has joined them;
   they are the forces of the children of Lot.

9 Treat them like Midian and Sisera
   like Jabin at the river Kishon.
10 They were destroyed at En-dor,
   they became as manure for the ground.

11 Treat their nobles like Oreb and Zeeb,
   all their rulers like Zebah and Zalmunna.
12 For they said, "Let us take for ourselves
   the finest of God's pastures."
13 O my God, treat them like whirling dust,
   like chaff before the wind.

14 As fire devours a forest,
   as a flame sets mountains ablaze,

15 so pursue them with Your tempest
    and terrify them with Your hurricane!
16 Fill their faces with shame,
    and they will seek Your Name, O Yahweh.

17 Let them be ashamed and terrified for ever;
    let them be confounded and perish.
18 Let them know—Your Name is Yahweh—
    that You alone are the Most High over all the earth.

PSALM 84
Desire for God's Sanctuary: A Pilgrim Song

To the choir director: on an instrument of Gath.
A Psalm of the Korahites.

1 How lovely is Your dwelling,
   O Yahweh Sabaoth!
2 My whole being longs and pines
   for Your courts, O Yahweh!
   My heart and flesh shout for joy
   to You, O living God!

3 Even the sparrow has found a home,
   the swallow a nest to place its young:
   Your altars, Yahweh Sabaoth,
   Adonai and my God!
4 Blessed are they who dwell in Your house,
   they shall always sing Your praises!

5 Blessed are they who find their strength in You,
   whose hearts are set on pilgrimage.
6 Passing through the valley of weeping
   they make it a place of springs;
   the early rain clothes it with abundance.

7 They go from company to company,
   to appear before God in Zion.
8 O Yahweh, God Sabaoth, hear my prayer,
   give ear, O God of Jacob!

9　Behold, O God our Shield,
　　look upon the face of Your anointed!
10　How much better is one day in Your courts
　　than a thousand of my own choice;
　　to stand on the threshold of God's house
　　than to live in the tents of the wicked.

11　Truly Sun and Defender,
　　Yahweh God bestows grace and glory.
　　Yahweh refuses nothing good
　　to those who walk in just ways.
12　O Yahweh Sabaoth,
　　blessed are those who trust in You!

PSALM 85
Prayer for Peace and Justice

To the choir director. A Psalm of the Korahites.

1　Yahweh, You have been gracious to Your land,
　　You have brought back the captives of Jacob.
2　You have forgiven the guilt of Your people;
　　You have blotted out all their sin.
3　You have withdrawn all Your wrath;
　　You have revoked Your burning anger.

4　Return to us, O God our Saviour,
　　appease Your indignation against us!
5　Will You be angry with us for ever?
　　Will you prolong Your wrath age after age?

6　Will You not restore and revive us again,
　　that Your people may rejoice in You?
7　Show us Your faithful love, O Yahweh,
　　and grant us Your salvation.

8　Let me announce what Yahweh God has promised:
　　You have promised peace to Your people,
　　to Your faithful ones, O Yahweh,
　　to those who turn to You in their hearts.

9   Your saving help is near to those who revere You,
Your glory will dwell in our land.

10   Compassionate love and faithfulness will meet;
justice and peace will kiss each other.

11   Faithfulness will spring up from the ground,
and justice will look down from heaven.

12   You, O Yahweh, will give what is good,
and our land will yield its increase.

13   Justice will march before You,
treading a way for Your footsteps.

PSALM 86
Humble Prayer for God's Mercy

A Prayer of David.

1   Incline Your ear, O Yahweh, and answer me,
for I am poor and needy.

2   Protect my life, for I am devoted to You,
save Your servant who trusts in You, my God.

3   Be gracious to me, O Adonai,
for to You do I cry out all day long.

4   Give joy to the soul of Your servant,
for to You, O Adonai, I lift up my soul.

5   For You are good and forgiving, O Adonai,
rich in faithful love to all who call on You.

6   O Yahweh, give ear to my prayer,
listen to my voice in supplication.

7   In the day of my distress I call on You,
O that You would answer me!

8   There is none like You among the gods, Adonai,
no great deeds to compare with Yours.

9   All nations that You have made will come
and prostrate themselves before You, O Adonai,
and they will glorify Your Name.

10 For You are great and do marvelous deeds,
   You alone are God.

11 Teach me Your way, O Yahweh,
   that I may walk in Your truth;
   teach my heart to revere Your Name.

12 I thank You with my whole heart,
   O Adonai, my God,
   and I will glorify Your Name for ever.
13 Great is Your faithful love toward me,
   and You have delivered my soul
   from the depths of Sheol.

14 O God, the arrogant have risen against me,
   a mob of the violent have sought my life,
   and have not set You before their eyes.

15 But You, O Adonai, are God,
   full of mercy, gracious, slow to anger,
   and rich in faithful love and fidelity.

16 Turn to me and be gracious to me;
   give Your servant Your strength,
   the child of Your servant Your saving help.

17 Give me a sign of Your favor, O Yahweh,
   that my enemies may see and be ashamed
   for You are my helper and my comforter.

PSALM 87
A Hymn in Praise of the City of God

A Psalm of the Korahites. A Song.

1 A city with its foundation
   on the holy mountain,
2 Yahweh loves You, O gates of Zion,
   more than all the dwellings of Jacob.

3 Glorious things are spoken of You,
  O city of God.

4 I will mention Rahab and Babylon,
  among those who acknowledge Me;
  behold, Philistia and Tyre, with Ethiopia:
  "This one was born there."

5 And of Zion it will be said,
  "This one and that one were born there;
  for the Most High will make it secure."

6 Yahweh will record,
  in the register of the peoples:
  "This one was born there."

7 Both singers and dancers alike say,
  "My home is within you."

PSALM 88
A Prayer for Help in Mortal Illness

A Song. A Psalm of the Korahites.
To the choir director: to the tune of "Mahalath Leannoth."
A Maskil—An Instruction of Heman the Ezrahite.

1 O Yahweh, God of my salvation,
  I cry out day and night before You.

2 Let my prayer come before You,
  incline Your ear to my supplication!

3 For my soul is filled with distress,
  and my life draws near to Sheol.

4 I am numbered with those who go down to the Pit;
  I am like those who have no strength,

5 like one left alone among the dead,
  like the slain that lie in the grave,
  like those whom You remember no more,
  for they are cut off from Your protection.

6 You have plunged me to the bottom of the Pit,
   in darkness and in the shadow of death.
7 Your wrath weighs heavy upon me,
   and You afflict me with all Your outbursts.

8 You have taken my companions away from me;
   You have made me an abomination to them.
   I am imprisoned that I cannot escape.
9 My eye wastes away because of affliction.

   Every day I call upon You, O Yahweh;
   I outstretch my hands to You.
10 Will You work wonders for the dead?
   Will the departed spirits rise to praise You?

11 Is Your faithful love declared in the grave,
   or Your faithfulness in Abaddon?
12 Are Your marvels known in the darkness,
   or Your generosity in the land of oblivion?

13 But I cry out to You, O Yahweh;
   at dawn let my prayer come before You.
14 O Yahweh, why do You rebuff me?
   Why do You turn Your face from me?

15 Distressed and close to death since childhood,
   I have borne Your afflictions; I am feeble.
16 Your outrage has overwhelmed me;
   Your onslaughts nearly destroyed me.

17 They surround me like a flood all day long;
   they engulfed me altogether.
18 You have taken from me lover and friend,
   the one who knows me well, into darkness.

PSALM 89
Hymn to God, the Rock of Deliverance

A Maskil—An Instruction of Ethan the Ezrahite.

1 I will sing of Your faithful love,
    O Yahweh, for ever;
    with my mouth I will proclaim
    Your faithfulness to all generations.
2 "Faithful love shall be established for ever,
    Your faithfulness is firm as the heavens."

3 You said, "I have made a covenant with My chosen,
    I have sworn to My servant David:
4 'I will establish your descendants for ever,
    and build your throne for all generations.' "

5 The heavens praise Your wonders, O Yahweh,
    Your constancy in the assembly of Your faithful!
6 Who in the skies can be compared to Yahweh?
    Who among the heavenly beings resembles Yahweh?

7 God, awesome in the assembly of the holy ones,
    great and revered above all that are around.
8 O Yahweh God Sabaoth, who is like You?
    Mighty Yahweh, Your faithfulness surrounds You.

9 You rule the splendor of the sea;
    when its waves rise, You still them.
10 You crushed Rahab like a carcass,
    with Your strong arm You scattered Your foes.

11 Yours are the heavens, Yours are the earth;
    the world and all it holds, You founded them.
12 You created Zaphon and Amanus,
    Tabor and Hermon joyously praise Your Name.

13 Yours is the arm, Yours is the might;
    Your hand is strong, Your right hand is exalted.
14 Truth and justice are the foundation of Your throne;
    faithful love and fidelity go before You.

15 Happy are the people who know Your radiance,
    who walk, O Yahweh, in the light of Your face.
16 They rejoice in Your Name all day long,
    and in Your saving justice they are exalted

17 For You are the glory of their strength;
    by Your favor You give us victory.
18 Truly Yahweh is our Shield,
    the Holy One of Israel is our Ruler.

19 Once You spoke in a vision,
    to Your faithful one You said:
    "I have set the crown upon one who is mighty,
    I have exalted one chosen from My people.

20 I have found David, My servant;
    I have anointed him with My holy oil.
21 My hand shall always be with him,
    My arm will make him strong.

22 The enemy will not prevail upon him,
    the wicked shall not humble him.
23 I will crush his enemies before him
    and strike down those who hate him.

24 My fidelity and faithful love shall be with him,
    in My Name his strength shall be exalted.
25 I shall establish his power over the sea
    and his right hand on the rivers.

26 He shall cry to Me, 'You are Abba, my God,
    the Rock of my deliverance.'
27 I will make him the first-born,
    the greatest of the rulers of the earth.

28 I will keep My faithful love for him for ever,
    and My covenant will stand firm for him.
29 I will establish his line for ever,
    his throne to be lasting as the heavens.

30 Should his descendants forsake My law
    and not walk according to My ordinances,
31 should they violate My laws
    and not observe My commandments,

32 then I will punish their offenses with the rod
    and their wrongdoing with scourges;
33 but I will not withdraw from him My faithful love,
    nor allow My faithfulness to fail.

34 I will not violate My covenant,
    nor alter the word that has gone out of My lips.
35 I have sworn by My holiness, once and for all,
    never will I break faith with David.

36 His descendants shall endure for ever,
    his throne as long as the sun before Me.
37 Like the moon it shall be established for ever;
    it shall stand firm while the skies endure.''

38 ''But now You have forsaken me and rejected me,
    You are full of wrath against Your anointed.
39 You have repudiated the covenant with Your servant;
    You have cast off my crown to the ground.

40 You have broken down all my walls;
    You have laid my strongholds in ruins.
41 All that pass by the way plunder me;
    I have become the scorn of my neighbors.

42 You have exalted the right hand of my enemies;
    You have made my enemies rejoice.
43 Yea, You have turned back the edge of my sword,
    and You have not made me stand in battle.

44 You have removed the scepter from my hand,
    and cast my throne to the ground.
45 You have cut short the days of my youth;
    You have covered me with shame.

46 How long, Yahweh, will You remain hidden? For ever?
    How long will Your wrath burn like fire?
47 Remember, O Yahweh, what the measure of life is,
    for what vanity You have created all humanity!
48 Who among the living never see death?
    Who can deliver their soul from the power of Sheol?

49 Adonai, where is Your faithful love of old,
    the faithful promises You made to David?
50 Remember, Adonai, how Your servant is scorned;
    how I bear in my bosom the insults of the peoples,
51 with which Your enemies taunt, O Yahweh,
    with which they mock the footsteps of Your anointed."

52 Blessed be Yahweh for ever!
    Amen and Amen.

BOOK FOUR
Psalms 90–106

PSALM 90
A Prayer of Moses, the Servant of God

A Prayer of Moses, the servant of God.

1 O Adonai, You have been our refuge,
   through all generations.
2 Before the mountains were brought forth,
   before the earth and the world came to birth,
   from eternity to eternity You are God.

3 You turn humans back to dust,
   and say, "Turn back, O mortal being!"
4 A thousand years are to You,
   like a yesterday which has passed,
   like a watch of the night.

5 The span of their life is like a dream,
     the next morning they are like changing grass;
6 which at dawn sprouts and shoots up;
     in the evening it withers and dries up.

7 For we are consumed by Your anger;
     we are troubled by Your wrath.
8 You have kept our offenses before You,
     the sins of our youth in the light of Your face.

9 For all our days pass away in Your wrath,
     our years come to an end like a sigh.
10 The span of our life is seventy years,
     and eighty for those who are strong,
     but their whole extent is anxiety and trouble;
     they are over in a moment, and we are gone.

11 Who feels the power of Your anger,
     and the fear of Your wrath?

12 So teach us to number our days
     that we may apply our hearts to wisdom.
13 Come back, O Yahweh! How long?
     Have compassion on Your servants!

14 Fill us at daybreak with Your faithful love,
     that we may sing and be happy all our days.
15 Make us glad according to the days of our affliction
     the years in which we have seen evil.

16 Let Your work be manifested to Your servants,
     and Your splendor to their children.
17 Let the benevolence of Yahweh our God be upon us,
     and may Yahweh sustain the work of our hands,
     O yes, strengthen the work of our hands.

PSALM 91
A Royal Psalm of Trust in Yahweh

1 You who dwell in the shelter of the Most High,
   spend the nights in the shadow of Shaddai,
2 say "O Yahweh, my refuge and my fortress;
   my God, in Whom I trust."

3 Yahweh will rescue you from the snare of the fowler
   and shield you from the venomous gossip.
4 With pinions God will cover You,
   under God's wings you will find refuge;
   God's faithfulness shall be a shield and guard.

5 You shall not fear the terrors of night,
   nor the arrow that flies in the daytime,
6 nor the pestilence that stalks in darkness,
   nor the destruction that devour at high noon.

7 Though a thousand may fall at your side,
   ten thousand at your right hand;
   it shall not come near you.
8 You have only to keep your eyes open
   to see how the wicked are repaid.

9 Because you say, 'O Yahweh my Refuge,'
   and make the Most High your habitation,
10 no misfortune shall overtake you,
   no scourge shall come near your dwelling.

11 For Yahweh has given angels charge over you
   to guard you in all your ways.
12 They shall bear you up in their palms,
   lest you dash your foot against a stone.

13 You shall tread upon viper and adder,
   you shall trample young lions and serpents.
14 "Because you cleave to Me in love,
   I will rescue you;
   I will protect you, because you know My Name.

137

15   When you call to Me, I will answer you,
       I will be with you in time of distress,
       I will rescue you and honor you.
16   With long life I will satisfy you,
       and grant you to see My salvation."

PSALM 92
A Song for the Sabbath

A Psalm. A Song for the Sabbath.

1   It is good to give thanks to Yahweh,
       to sing praises to Your Name, O Most High;
2   to proclaim Your faithful love at daybreak,
       and Your faithfulness all through the night,
3   to the music of the zither and the harp,
       to the melody of the lyre.

4   For You made me joyful by Your work, O Yahweh;
       at the work of Your hands I sing for joy.
5   How great are Your works, O Yahweh!
       How profound are Your thoughts!
6   The senseless ones cannot comprehend,
       the stupid ones cannot understand it.

7   The wicked may sprout like weeds
       every evildoer may flourish,
       they are for ever doomed to destruction.
8   But You, O Yahweh,
       are the Exalted for ever.
9   Look, how all Your enemies perish, O Yahweh,
       how all evildoers are scattered.

10   You exalted my horn like the wild ox;
       You anoint me with refreshing oil.
11   My eyes saw the defeat of my adversaries,
       my ears heard the doom of my assailants.

138

12 The just shall flourish like the palm tree,
   and shall grow like the cedar of Lebanon.

13 Those planted in the house of Yahweh,
   in the courts of our God, shall flourish.
14 They shall still bear fruit in old age,
   they shall remain fresh and flourishing.
15 They proclaim that Yahweh, my Rock, is just,
   in Whom there is no injustice.

PSALM 93
A Hymn Celebrating Yahweh's Reign

1 Yahweh reigns, clothed with majesty,
   Yahweh is robed with might.
   Yahweh is girded with strength.

   The world is established;
   it shall never be shaken.
2 Your throne is established from of old;
   You are from eternity.

3 The floods have lifted up, O Yahweh,
   the floods have lifted up their voices,
   the floods lift up their roaring waves.

4 Yahweh on high is mightier
   than the thunder of many waters,
   mightier than the waves of the sea.

5 O Yahweh, Your decrees are very sure,
   and holiness befits Your house for ever.

PSALM 94
A Psalm of Thanksgiving to the God of Justice

1 O Yahweh God, to Whom vindication belongs,
   O God, to Whom vindication belongs, show Yourself.

2 Rise up, O Judge of the earth;
   render to the proud what they deserve!

3 How long shall the wicked, Yahweh,
   how long shall the wicked triumph?
4 They explode and speak imprudent things,
   they speak proudly, all workers of evil.

5 They crush Your people, O Yahweh,
   and oppress Your heritage.
6 They murder the widow and the sojourner,
   and bring the orphan to a violent death.

7 They say, "Yahweh does not see;
   the God of Israel does not perceive."
8 Understand, you beastly ones of the people;
   and you fools, when will you be wise?

9 Shall the One Who planted the ear not hear?
   Shall the One Who formed the eye not see?
10 Shall the instructor of nations not chastise?
   Shall the teacher of people be without knowledge?
11 Yahweh knows human plans and that they are vain.

12 Blessed are those whom You chasten, O Yahweh,
   and whom You teach by means of Your law,
13 to give them rest from troubled days,
   until a pit is dug for the wicked.

14 You, O Yahweh will not forsake Your people;
   You will not abandon Your heritage;
15 for justice will return to the just,
   and all the just in heart will follow it.

16 Who will rise up for me against the wicked?
   Who will stand up for me against evildoers?
17 If Yahweh had not been my help,
   my soul would have dwelt in the land of silence.

18 When I said, "My foot slips,"
   Your faithful love, O Yahweh, held me up.

19 When the anxieties of my heart are many,
    Your consolations comfort my soul.

20 Can wicked rulers be allied with You,
    those who contrive mischief against Your law?
21 They band together against the life of the just,
    and condemn the innocent blood.

22 But Yahweh has become my stronghold,
    and my God the Rock of my refuge.
23 Yahweh will turn back on them their evil,
    and wipe them out for their wickedness;
    Yahweh our God will annihilate them.

PSALM 95
A Hymn Celebrating Yahweh's Reign

1 O come, let us sing joyfully to Yahweh;
   let us acclaim the Rock of our salvation!
2 Let us come into God's presence with thanksgiving;
   let us acclaim God with songs of praise!

3 For Yahweh is a great God,
   and a great Ruler above all gods.
4 In Whose hand are the depths of the earth;
   and Yahweh's are the peaks of the mountains.
5 The sea belongs to Yahweh, its maker;
   and it was God Who formed the dry land.

6 O come, let us worship and bow down,
   let us kneel before Yahweh, our Maker!
7 For Yahweh is our God,
   and we are the people of God's pasture,
   and the flock God guides.

   "Oh that today you would hear my voice:
8 Harden not your hearts, as at Meribah,
   as on the day at Massah in the wilderness,

9   when your ancestors challenged me,
     tested me, though they had seen my works.

10   For forty years I was grieved with this generation,
     and I said, 'They are a people who err in heart,
     and they do not know My ways.'
11   Therefore I swore in My anger,
     'They shall not enter into My rest.' "

PSALM 96
A Hymn Celebrating Yahweh's Sovereignty

1   Sing to Yahweh a new song;
     sing to Yahweh, all the earth!

2   Sing to Yahweh, bless God's Name;
     proclaim God's salvation day after day.
3   Declare God's glory among the nations,
     the marvelous works among all the peoples!

4   For great is Yahweh, and greatly to be praised;
     Who is to be revered above all gods.
5   For all the gods of the nations are idols;
     but it was Yahweh Who made the heavens.

6   Before Yahweh are splendor and majesty;
     strength and beauty are in God's sanctuary.
7   Give to Yahweh, O families of the peoples,
     give to Yahweh glory and strength!

8   Give to Yahweh the glory due the Name;
     bring an offering, and come into the Presence!
9   Worship Yahweh in the splendor of holiness;
     tremble before God, all the earth!

10   Say among the nations, "Yahweh reigns!
     The world is set firm, it cannot be moved.
     Yahweh will judge nations with justice."

11 Let the heavens be glad, and the earth rejoice;
let the sea roar, and all it holds!

12 Let the fields exult, and all that is in it;
and all the trees of the forest sing for joy,

13 before the coming of Yahweh,
for Yahweh comes to judge the earth.
Yahweh will judge the world with justice,
and the nations with constancy.

PSALM 97
A Hymn Celebrating Yahweh,
the Universal Judge

1 Yahweh reigns; let the earth rejoice;
let the many isles be glad!

2 Clouds and thick darkness enfold You;
integrity and justice are
the foundations of Your throne.

3 A fire goes before You,
and burns up Your foes all around.

4 Your lightning lights up the world;
the earth sees it and trembles.

5 The mountains melt like wax before Yahweh,
before the God of all the earth.

6 The heavens proclaim Your saving justice;
and all the nations see Your glory.

7 All who worship images are put to shame,
and those who boast in worthless idols;
all gods prostrate before You.

8 Zion hears and is glad,
and the cities of Judah rejoice,
because of Your judgments, O Yahweh.

9 For You are Yahweh,
   Most High over all the earth;
   You are exalted far above all gods.

10 Yahweh, You love those who hate evil;
    You preserve the lives of Your saints;
    You deliver them from the hand of the wicked.

11 Light dawns for the just,
    and joy for the honest in heart.
12 Rejoice in Yahweh, O you just,
    and give thanks to God's holy Name!

PSALM 98
A Hymn Praising Yahweh's Eternal Rule

A Psalm.

1 Sing a new song to Yahweh,
   Who has done marvelous things!
   In Whose right hand,
   in Whose holy arm is saving power.

2 Yahweh, You have made known Your victory,
   You have revealed Your justice for all to see.
3 You have remembered Your faithful love
   and constancy to the house of Israel.

   All the ends of the earth have seen
   the saving power of our God.
4 Sing joyfully to Yahweh, all the earth;
   break forth into joyous song and sing praises!

5 Sing praises to Yahweh with the lyre,
   with the lyre and the sound of melody!
6 With trumpets and the sound of the horn
   sing joyfully before Yahweh the Ruler!

7 Let the sea roar, and all that fills it;
   the world and those who dwell in it!

8   Let the floods clap their hands;
    let the hills sing for joy together

9   Rejoice before Yahweh, Who comes to judge the earth.
    Yahweh will judge the world with justice,
    and the peoples with equity.

PSALM 99
A Hymn in Praise of Yahweh's Reign

1   Yahweh reigns,
    let the peoples tremble!
    Yahweh is enthroned upon the cherubim,
    let the earth quake!

2   "Yahweh, You are too great for Zion;
    You are exalted over all the peoples.
3   Let them praise Your great and awesome Name!
    Holy are You!

4   O Mighty Ruler, lover of justice,
    You Yourself have established equity;
    You have executed justice and integrity in Jacob."

5   Extol Yahweh our God;
    Worship at God's footstool!
    Holy is God!

6   "Moses and Aaron were among Your priests,
    Samuel was among those who called on Your Name.
    They cried to You Yahweh, and You answered them.

7   You spoke to them in the pillar of cloud;
    they obeyed Your decrees and the laws You gave them.
8   O Yahweh our God, You Yourself answered them;
    You were God of forgiveness to them,
    and You cleansed them of their sins."

9 Extol Yahweh our God,
   Worship at God's holy mountain;
   Holy is Yahweh our God!

PSALM 100
A Song of Praise to Yahweh, Our Maker

A Psalm for thanksgiving.

1 Acclaim Yahweh, all the earth!
2 Serve Yahweh with gladness!
   Come before God with joyful songs!

3 Know that Yahweh is God,
   we belong to Yahweh our Maker,
   we are God's people,
   the sheep of God's pasture.

4 Come into God's gates with thanksgiving,
   and to the courts with songs of praise!
   Give thanks and bless God's Name!

5 For Yahweh is good;
   Whose faithful love is everlasting,
   Whose faithfulness to all generations.

PSALM 101
Royal Psalm on Faithfulness and Justice

A Psalm of David.

1 I will sing of mercy and justice;
   to You, Yahweh, will I sing praise!
2 I will walk in the path of integrity;
   Oh when will You come to me?

   I will live with integrity of heart
   in the midst of my house;
3 I will not set before my eyes
   anything that is vicious.

I hate the ways of the perverse;
they shall not come near to me.

4 The wicked of heart shall be far from me;
I disregard the ones with malice.

5 Whoever secretly slanders a neighbor
I will reduce to silence.
Those of haughty looks and proud heart
I will not condone.

6 I will seek out the faithful of the land,
to dwell with me in my house.
Those who walk in the way of justice,
shall be in my service.

7 No one who practices deceit
shall dwell in my house.
No one who utters falsehood
shall continue in my presence.

8 In the mornings I will silence
the wicked of the land.
From the city of Yahweh,
I will destroy the evildoers.

PSALM 102
Hymn to Yahweh's Eternal Love
Fifth Penitential Psalm

1 Hear my prayer, O Yahweh;
let my cry come to You!
2 Do not hide Your face from me
in the day of my trouble!
Incline Your ear toward me;
when I call, hasten to answer me!

3 For my days vanish like smoke,
my bones burn like a furnace.

147

4 Like grass struck by blight,
   my heart is withering.
   I forget to eat my bread.
5 Because of my loud groaning
   my bones cleave to my flesh.

6 I am like a vulture of the wilderness,
   like an owl of the waste places;
7 I lie awake and moan,
   like a sparrow alone on a roof.
8 All day long my enemies insult me,
   those who once praised me,
   now swear against me.

9 For I eat ashes like bread,
   my drink is mingled with tears.
10 Because of Your fury and wrath,
   You have lifted me and cast me down.
11 My days are like a fading shadow,
   I wither away like grass.

12 But You, Yahweh, remain for ever;
   Your remembrance to all generations.
13 Rise up and have mercy on Zion;
   the time has come to have mercy on Zion;
   the appointed time has come.
14 For Your servants hold its very stones dear,
   are moved to pity by the dust within it.

15 The nations will revere Your Name, O Yahweh,
   all the rulers of the earth Your glory.
16 When You, Yahweh, build up Zion anew,
   You appear to her in Your glory.
17 You regard the prayer of the destitute,
   and do not despise their supplication.

18 Let this be recorded for the generations to come,
   that a people yet unborn may praise Yahweh.

19 "Yahweh looked down from the holy height
   from heaven gazed to the earth,
20 to hear the groans of the prisoners,
   to release those condemned to die,
21 to declare the name of Yahweh in Zion
   and praises of Yahweh in Jerusalem,
22 when peoples gather together,
   with their rulers to serve Yahweh."

23 Yahweh has weakened my strength on earth,
   and warned me of cutting short my days.
24 "O my God," I said,
   "do not take me hence in the midst of my days,
   when Your years endure for generations!"

25 Long ago You laid foundations of the earth,
   the heavens are the work of Your hands.
26 They will perish, but You remain;
   they will all wear out like a garment,
   as a vesture You shall fold them,
   and they shall be changed;
27 but You remain the same,
   and Your years shall never end.

28 Your servants' children shall dwell secure;
   their posterity shall prosper for ever.

PSALM 103
Hymn of Praise for Yahweh's Mercies

A Psalm of David.

1 Bless Yahweh, O my soul;
  and all my being, bless God's Holy Name!
2 Bless Yahweh, O my soul,
  and forget not all God's benefits,

3 in forgiving all your offenses,
  in healing all your diseases,

4 in redeeming your life from destruction,
   in crowning you with mercy and compassion,
5 in satisfying your desires with good things
   and in renewing your youth like the eagle's.

6 Yahweh acts with integrity
   with justice to all who are oppressed,
7 Yahweh's ways were revealed to Moses,
   and acts to the people of Israel.

8 Yahweh is merciful and gracious,
   slow to anger and rich in faithful love.
9 Yahweh will not punish us for ever,
   nor will Yahweh be angry for ever.
10 Yahweh does not treat us as our sins deserve,
   nor avenge us according to our iniquities.

11 For as the heavens are high above the earth,
   so great is Your faithful love
   toward those who revere You;
12 as far as the east is from the west,
   so far You remove our offenses from us.

13 As tenderly as parents treat their children,
   so You, Yahweh, treat those who revere You.
14 For You know how we are made;
   You remember that we are dust.

15 As for humans, their days are like grass;
   they flourish like flowers of the field;
16 as soon as the wind blows they are gone,
   never to be seen there again.

17 Your faithful love toward those who revere You,
   is from eternity to eternity, O Yahweh,
   Your justice to their children's children,
18 to those who keep Your covenant
   and remember to fulfill Your precepts.

19 Yahweh has set the throne in heaven,
   and God's dominion rules over all.
20 Bless Yahweh, O you angels,
   you mighty ones who fulfill God's word,
   attentive to the word of command!

21 Bless Yahweh, all you hosts,
   you ministers who fulfill God's wishes!
22 Bless Yahweh, all you creatures,
   in every place where Yahweh rules.
   Bless Yahweh, O my soul!

PSALM 104
Hymn of Praise to God the Creator

1 Bless Yahweh, O my soul!
   Yahweh my God, You are great indeed!
   You are clothed with honor and majesty,
2 covering Yourself with light like a cloak.

   You stretch out the heavens like a tent,
3 build Your chambers on the waters above.
   You make the clouds Your chariot,
   You ride on the wings of the wind.
4 You make the winds Your messengers,
   fire and flame Your ministers.

5 You fixed the earth on its foundations,
   so that it should never be shaken.
6 You covered it with the deep like a garment,
   the waters stood above the mountains.

7 At Your rebuke the waters fled,
   at the sound of Your thunder they sped away.
8 The mountains rose, the valleys sank down
   to the place which You had fixed for them.
9 You set a limit which they should not pass,
   so that they might not again cover the earth.

10 You make springs gush forth in the valleys,
    running down between the mountains,
11 giving drink to every animal of the field,
    that the wild asses may quench their thirst.

12 Near them the birds of the air dwell;
    they sing their songs among the branches.
13 From Your heavenly home You water the mountains,
    satisfying the earth with the fruit of Your works.

14 You cause the grass to grow for the cattle,
    and for people the plants they need,
    to bring forth grain from the earth,
15 wine to cheer people's hearts,
    oil to make their faces glow,
    bread to sustain their hearts.

16 Well watered are Your trees, O Yahweh,
    the cedars of Lebanon which You planted.
17 In them the birds build their nests,
    in the fir trees the stork make their homes.
18 The high mountains are home for wild goats,
    the cliffs are a refuge for badgers.

19 You made the moon to mark the seasons,
    the sun knows its hour for setting.
20 You make darkness, and night comes on,
    when all the forest beasts roam around.
21 The young lions roar for their prey,
    asking God for their food.

22 When the sun rises, they steal away,
    and go to their dens to lie down.
23 People go forth to their work
    to labor till evening falls.

24 O Yahweh, how manifold are Your works!
    You have made them all in wisdom.
    The earth is full of Your creatures.

25 Then there is the sea, great and wide,
which teems with countless creatures,
living things both small and great.
26 There the ships pass to and fro
and Leviathan whom You formed to sport with.

27 All of them look to You,
to give them their food in due season.
28 You provide the food they gather,
You open Your hand and give them their fill.

29 You turn away Your face, they panic;
You take away Your Spirit, they die,
and return to their dust.
30 You send out Your Spirit, they are created;
and You renew the face of the earth.

31 May the glory of Yahweh endure for ever,
may You, Yahweh, find joy in Your works.
32 You gaze upon the earth and it trembles,
You touch the mountains and they smoke!

33 I will sing to Yahweh all my life;
I will praise my God as long as I live.

34 May my musings be pleasing to Yahweh,
for Yahweh gives me joy.
35 May sinners vanish from the earth,
and may the wicked exist no more!
Bless Yahweh, O my soul!
Praise Yahweh!

PSALM 105
Hymn of Praise to God the Ever Faithful

1 We give You thanks, O Yahweh,
we call on Your Name,
we proclaim Your deeds to the nations!

2   We sing to You,
    we sing praises to You,
    we chant of all Your wonderful works!

3   We glory in Your holy Name;
    let the hearts of all who seek Yahweh rejoice!
4   We seek You, Yahweh, and Your strength,
    we constantly seek Your Presence!

5   "Remember the wonders Yahweh has done,
    the miracles and judgments of Yahweh,
6   O stock of Abraham, Yahweh's servant,
    children of Jacob, Yahweh's chosen one!"

7   You are Yahweh our God;
    Your judgments are in all the earth.
8   You are mindful of Your covenant for ever,
    of the word that You commanded,
    for a thousand generations,
9   the covenant which You made with Abraham,
    Your sworn promise to Isaac,
10 which You confirmed to Jacob as a law,
    to Israel as an everlasting covenant,

11 saying, "To you I will give the land,
    Canaan, as your portion for an inheritance."

12 When they were insignificant in numbers,
    a handful of strangers in the land,
13 wandering from country to country,
    from one territory and nation to another,

14 You allowed no one to oppress them;
    You rebuked rulers on their account,
15 saying, "Touch not my anointed ones,
    and do no harm to my prophets!"

16 When You summoned a famine on the land,
    and broke every stalk of grain,

17   You sent one ahead of them,
     Joseph, who was sold as a slave.

18   His feet were bound with fetters,
     and his neck was put in irons;
19   until what You had said came to pass,
     Your word, O Yahweh, tested him.

20   The ruler sent orders to unbind him,
     sovereign of the nations set him free;
21   and made him chief over the household,
     and ruler of all his possessions,

22   to instruct his princes at his pleasure,
     and to teach his elders wisdom.
23   Then Israel migrated to Egypt;
     Jacob sojourned in the land of Ham.

24   You, Yahweh, made Your people very fruitful,
     made them stronger than their enemies.
25   You turned their hearts to hate Your people,
     to deal craftily with Your own servants.

26   You sent Moses Your servant,
     and Aaron whom You had chosen.
27   They wrought Your signs among them,
     and miracles in the land of Ham.

28   You sent darkness, and made the land dark,
     but they rebelled against Your words.
29   You turned their waters into blood,
     and caused their fish to die.

30   Their country was overrun with frogs,
     even in the chambers of their rulers.
31   You spoke, and there came swarms of flies,
     and gnats throughout their country.

32   You gave them hail as their rain,
     flames of fire in their land.

33 You blasted their vines and fig trees,
    and shattered the trees of the country.

34 You spoke, and the locusts came,
    and grasshoppers without number;
35 they devoured all the vegetation of the land,
    and ate up the fruit of their ground.

36 You struck all the first-born in their land,
    the first issue of all their strength.
37 You led forth Israel with silver and gold,
    and none among Your tribes stumbled.

38 Egypt was glad at their leaving,
    for dread of Israel had fallen upon it.
39 You spread a cloud for a covering,
    and fire to give light by night.

40 They asked, and You brought them quails,
    and gave them bread from heaven in abundance.
41 You opened the rock, and water gushed forth;
    it flowed through the desert like a river.

42 For You remembered Your holy promise,
    given to Abraham Your servant.
43 So You led forth Your people with joy,
    Your chosen ones with shouts of joy.

44 You gave them the lands of the nations,
    and they inherited the labor of the peoples,
45 on condition that they kept Your statutes,
    and remained obedient to Your laws.

    Praise Yahweh!

PSALM 106
Joy in Confession and Forgiveness of Sins

1   Praise Yahweh!

   O give thanks to Yahweh, Who is good;
   Whose faithful love endures for ever!

2   Who can recount all Yahweh's triumphs
   or fully declare Yahweh's praise?

3   Blessed are they who observe justice,
   and they that do justice at all times!

4   Remember me, O Yahweh,
   in Your love for Your people;
   come visit me with Your saving help;

5   that I may enjoy
   the prosperity of Your chosen ones,
   share the joy of Your people,
   glory in Your inheritance.

6   We have sinned like our ancestors;
   we have done wrong, committed crimes.

7   Our ancestors in Egypt never perceived
   the meaning of Your wonders,
   they remembered not Your abounding love,
   but defied the Most High at the Sea of Reeds.

8   Yet You saved them for Your Name's sake,
   that You might make known Your mighty power.

9   You rebuked the Red Sea, and it became dry;
   You led them through the deep as through a desert.

10   So You saved them from the hands of the foe,
   and freed them from the power of the enemy.

11   The waters covered their adversaries;
   not one of them was left.

12   Then they believed Your words;
   and they sang Your praise.

13 But they soon forgot Your works;
    they trusted not in Your counsel.
14 But they complained bitterly in the desert,
    and tested You, El, in the barrens.

15 Yet You gave them their request,
    and You supplied them with abundance.
16 They plotted against Moses in the camp
    and Aaron, the holy one of Yahweh.

17 The earth opened and swallowed up Dathan,
    and covered the company of Abiram.
18 A fire was kindled in their company;
    the flame burned up the wicked.

19 They made a calf in Horeb
    and worshiped a molten image.
20 They exchanged their Glorious One
    for the image of a grass-eating bull.

21 They forgot God, their Deliverer,
    Who had done great things in Egypt,
22 wonders in the land of Ham,
    awesome things by the Red Sea.

23 Therefore You said You would destroy them,
    had not Moses, Your chosen one,
    stood before You in the breach,
    to turn away Your wrath from destroying them.

24 Then they rejected the desirable land,
    having no faith in Your promise.
25 They murmured in their tents,
    and hearkened not the voice of Yahweh.

26 Therefore You raised Your hand against them
    and made them fall in the wilderness,
27 and dispersed their descendants among the nations,
    scattering them over the lands.

28   They worshiped the idols of Baal-Peor,
     and ate sacrifices offered for the dead.
29   They provoked You to anger by their actions,
     that a plague broke out among them.

30   Then Phinehas stood up to intervene,
     and the plague was checked;
31   for this is the example of righteousness,
     for endless generations to come.

32   They angered You at the waters of Meribah,
     that Moses fared ill on their account;
33   for they made Your Spirit bitter,
     and You spoke words that were rash.

34   They did not destroy the peoples,
     as You, Yahweh, commanded them,
35   but they mingled with the nations
     and adopted their way of life.

36   They worshiped those nations' idols,
     till they found themselves entrapped.
37   They sacrificed their own sons
     and their daughters to the demons.

38   They poured out innocent blood,
     the blood of their sons and daughters;
     offering them to the idols of Canaan,
     they polluted the country with blood.

39   They defiled themselves by their actions,
     and prostituted themselves in their doings.
40   Then Your anger was kindled against Your people,
     You were disgusted with Your own heritage.

41   You handed them over to the nations,
     so that their enemies ruled over them.
42   Their enemies oppressed them,
     and subjected them to their power.

43 Time and again You delivered them,
     but they were rebellious in their purpose,
     and sank ever deeper in their wickedness.

44 Even so You took pity on their distress,
     as soon as You heard their cry for help.

45 You remembered Your covenant and pitied them,
     and relented in Your boundless and faithful love.

46 You caused them to be pitied
     by all those who held them captive.

47 Save us, O Yahweh our God,
     and gather us from among the nations,
     that we may give thanks to Your holy Name
     and glory in Your praise.

48 Blessed be Yahweh, the God of Israel,
     from everlasting to everlasting!
     And let all the people say, "Amen!"
     Praise Yahweh!

BOOK FIVE
Psalms 107–150

PSALM 107
Hymn of National Thanksgiving
for God's Kindness

1 O give thanks to Yahweh, Who is good;
    Whose faithful love endures for ever!

2 Let those redeemed by Yahweh say
    that Yahweh redeemed them from their foes

3   and gathered them from foreign lands:
    from the east and from the west,
    from the north and from the south.

4   Wandering in the wilderness and deserts,
    and finding no way to an inhabited town,
5   they became hungry and thirsty,
    and their spirit fainted within them.

6   In their distress they cried to Yahweh,
    Who delivered them from their woes;
7   and guided them in the straight way,
    till they reached a town to dwell in.

8   Let these confess to Yahweh God's faithful love,
    and to all peoples God's wonderful deeds!
9   For Yahweh satisfies the longing soul
    and fills with goodness the hungry soul.

10 Dwelling in darkness and in deep shadow,
    prisoners in affliction and iron,
11 They murmured against the words of God,
    and despised the counsel of the Most High.
12 Their hearts were humbled by hardship;
    and they stumbled, with none to help them.

13 In their distress they cried to Yahweh
    Who delivered them from their woes;
14 brought them out of gloom and shadow,
    and shattered their chains.

15 Let these confess to Yahweh God's faithful love,
    and to all peoples God's wonderful deeds!
16 For Yahweh shatters the doors of bronze,
    and cuts in two the bars of iron.

17 Fooled by their rebellious conduct,
    afflicted because of their iniquities,
18 they found every kind of food repugnant
    and they drew near to the gates of death.

19 In their distress they cried to Yahweh,
    Who delivered them from their woes;
20 Who sent out a word to heal them,
    and delivered them from destruction.

21 Let these confess to Yahweh God's faithful love,
    and to all peoples God's wonderful deeds!
22 Let them offer thanksgiving sacrifices,
    and recount Yahweh's deeds in joyful songs!

23 Traversing the sea in ships,
    carrying on trade over the great waters,
24 they saw the deeds of Yahweh,
    the wondrous works in the deep.

25 Yahweh spoke and raised the stormy wind,
    which lifted the waves of the sea.
26 Up to the sky then down to the depths,
    their soul melted away in their peril.
27 They reeled and staggered like drunks,
    and all their skill was swallowed up.

28 In their distress they cried to Yahweh,
    Who delivered them from their woes;
29 Who changed the storm to a whisper,
    the waves that roared were hushed.
30 They rejoiced because they grew calm,
    and were guided to their desired haven.

31 Let them confess to Yahweh God's faithful love,
    and to all peoples God's wonderful deeds!
32 Let them extol Yahweh in the assembly of the people,
    offer praise in the assembly of the elders.

33 Yahweh turned rivers into a desert,
    water springs into parched ground,
34 a fruitful land into a salty desert,
    for the wickedness of those who dwelt therein.

35 Yahweh turned a desert into pools of water,
    a parched land into water springs.
36 And there let the hungry dwell,
    and they established a town to dwell in.

37 They sowed fields, and planted vineyards,
    and harvested a fruitful yield.
38 They multiplied with the blessing of Yahweh
    Who allowed not their cattle to diminish.

39 But when they were repressed and humbled
    through oppression, torment and evil,
40 You heaped humiliation upon the nobles
    and made them wander in trackless wastes.

41 You raised the needy up from affliction,
    and increased their families like flocks.
42 Let the just see and greatly rejoice,
    and the wicked shall clap their mouths shut.

43 Whoever is wise, will observe these things;
    they shall discern Yahweh's faithful love.

PSALM 108
Confident Prayer for Victory over Enemies

A Song. A Psalm of David.

1 My heart is steadfast, O God,
    my heart is steadfast!
    I will sing and make melody!
    Awake, my soul!
2 Awake, O harp and lyre!
    I will awake the dawn!

3 I will praise You among the peoples, Yahweh,
    I will sing praises to You among the nations.
4 For Your faithful love towers to the heavens,
    and Your faithfulness reaches the clouds.

5   Be exalted, O God, above the heavens!
    Let Your glory be over all the earth!

6   That Your beloved may be delivered,
    save with Your right hand, and answer me!

7   God has promised in his sanctuary:
    "With exultation I will divide up Shechem,
    and portion out the Vale of Succoth.

8   Gilead is mine; Manasseh is mine;
    Ephraim is my helmet; Judah my scepter.

9   Moab is my washbasin;
    upon Edom I cast my shoe;
    over Philistia I shout in triumph."

10 Who will bring me to the fortified city?
    Who will lead me to Edom?

11 But You, O God, will You reject us?
    Will You go forth, O God, with our armies.

12 O grant us help against our foes,
    for vain is human help!

13 With You, O God, we shall be victorious;
    You will trample down our enemies.

PSALM 109
Dreadful Imprecations against
Slanderous Foes

To the choir director. A Psalm of David.

1   Be not silent,
    O God of my praise!

2   The wicked and the deceitful,
    have opened their mouths against me,
    they pursue me with a lying tongue.

3   They beset me with words of hate,
    and attack me without cause.

4   In return for my love they accuse me,
    even as I make prayer for them.
5   So they reward me evil for good,
    and hatred for my love.

6   Appoint a wicked judge against them,
    let an accuser bring them to trial.
7   When they are tried,
    let them come forth guilty;
    let their prayers be counted as sin!

8   May their days be few,
    may others take their office!
9   May their children be orphans,
    and their wives widows!

10 May their children wander about and beg,
    and seek food out of their ruins.
11 May creditors seize all their goods,
    may strangers plunder their earnings!

12 Let there be none showing kindness to them,
    nor any to pity their orphaned children!
13 May their posterity be cut off,
    may their name be erased in the age to come!

14 Let their fathers' iniquity be remembered to Yahweh,
    let not the sins of their mothers be blotted out.
15 May their wickedness be always before Yahweh,
    and let their memory be cut off from the earth.

16 For they did not remember to show kindness,
    but tortured the poor and the needy
    and the broken-hearted to their death.
17 They loved to curse, let curses be heaped on them!
    They disliked blessing, may it be far from them!

18 Cursing has been the uniform they wore,
    may it soak into their body like water,
    like oil into their bones!

19 Let it be like a robe they wrap around them,
and like a sash which they always wear!

20 May this be Yahweh's reward for my accusers,
for those who speak evil against my soul!
21 O Yahweh, Adonai, treat them as Your Name
demands,
in Your generous faithful love, deliver me!

22 For I am poor and needy,
and my heart is stricken within me.
23 I am passing away like a fading shadow,
they have shaken me off like a locust.

24 My knees are feeble from lack of food,
my body grows lean for lack of fat.
25 I have become a reproach to my accusers;
they shake their heads at the sight of me.

26 Help me, Yahweh my God,
save me according to Your faithful love!
27 Let them know that Yours is a saving hand;
You, O Yahweh, have done it!

28 Let them curse, provided that You bless!
Let my assailants be put to shame;
may Your servant be glad!
29 May my accusers be clothed with shame;
and cover themselves in shame as with a robe!

30 I will greatly thank Yahweh with my lips;
I will praise Yahweh before all the people.
31 For Yahweh stands at the side of the needy,
to save them from those who condemn them to death.

PSALM 110
Reign of the Priestly Messiah

A Psalm of David.

1 Yahweh declared to the anointed:
"Sit enthroned at my right hand,
until I place your foes as your footstool."

2 Yahweh will stretch out the scepter of your power:
from Zion you will rule in the midst of your foes!

3 Yours has been royal dignity
from the day of your birth,
sacred honor from the womb,
from the dawn of your youth.

4 Yahweh has sworn and will not repent,
"You are a priest for ever
according to the order of Melchizedek."

5 Yahweh standing at your right hand,
will shatter rulers on the day of wrath;
6 shall judge the nations, heaping up corpses,
will shatter heads over the wide earth;
7 will drink from the brook by the wayside,
and therefore shall hold your head high.

PSALM 111
Hymn of Praise of the Goodness of Yahweh

1 Praise Yahweh.

I give thanks to You, Yahweh, with all my heart,
in the company and assembly of the just.
2 Great are Your works, O Yahweh,
to be pondered by all who delight in them.

3 Your works are full of majesty and luster
and Your justice endures for ever.

4   You have made a memorial of wonderful works;
    and You, Yahweh, are compassionate and merciful.

5   You provide food for those who revere You;
    and You are ever mindful of Your covenant.

6   You have shown Your people the power of Your
       works,
    in giving them the heritage of the nations.

7   The works of Your hands are faithful and just,
    all Your precepts are trustworthy.

8   They are established for ever and ever,
    to be performed with devotion and integrity.

9   You have sent deliverance to Your people;
    You have commanded Your covenant for ever.
    Holy and awesome is Your Name!

10   "The reverence of Yahweh is the root of wisdom;
    and wise are all those who practice it."
    Your praise, Yahweh, endures for ever!

PSALM 112
Blessed are the Just Who Revere Yahweh

1   Praise Yahweh.

    Blessed are those who revere Yahweh,
    and delight in God's commandments!

2   Their descendants will be powerful in the land;
    the generation of the just will be blessed.

3   Wealth and riches are in their house;
    and their justice stands firm for ever.

4   Light rises in the darkness for the just,
    who is gracious, merciful, and honest.

5   All goes well for those who lend generously
    and conduct their affairs with justice.

6   For all time to come the just will not stumble;
    for all time to come they will be remembered.

7   They are not afraid of bad tidings;
    their heart is firm, trusting in Yahweh.
8   Their heart is steady, they have no fear,
    though they look on their foes.

9   Lavishly they give to the poor;
    their justice stands firm for ever;
    their horn is exalted in honor.

10 The wicked see it and are provoked;
    they gnash their teeth and waste away;
    the greed of the wicked comes to nought.

PSALM 113
Hymn to Yahweh's Mercy and Compassion

1   Praise Yahweh!

    Praise, O servants of Yahweh,
    praise the Name of Yahweh!
2   Blessed be the Name of Yahweh
    henceforth and for evermore!
3   From the rising of the sun to its setting,
    praised be the Name of Yahweh!

4   Yahweh is high above all nations,
    Whose glory is above the heavens!
5   Who is like Yahweh our God,
    Whose throne is set on high,
6   but Who stoops to look down
    on the heavens and the earth?

7   Yahweh raises the poor from the dust,
    and lifts the needy out of the dunghill,
8   to make them sit with the nobles,
    with the nobles of the chosen people.

169

9   Yahweh gives the childless woman a family,
    making her the joyful mother of children.

PSALM 114
Passover Hymn

Praise Yahweh!

1   When Israel came forth from Egypt,
    from a people of unknown language,
2   Judah became God's sanctuary,
    Israel, the house of Jacob, God's dominion.

3   The sea fled at the sight,
    Jordan turned back.
4   The mountains skipped like rams,
    the hills like lambs.

5   Why is it, O sea, that you flee?
    O Jordan, that you turn back?
6   O mountains, that you skip like rams?
    O hills, like lambs?

7   Tremble, O earth, in the presence of Yahweh,
    in the presence of the God of Jacob,
8   Who turned the rock into a pool of water,
    the hard rock into a spring of water.

PSALM 115
A Hymn to the Omnipotent God of Israel

1   Not to us, O Yahweh, not to us,
    but to Your Name give the glory,
    because of Your love and faithfulness.
2   Why do the nations say,
    "Where is their God now?"

3   Our God is in the heavens;
    everything God wanted came to be.

4 Their idols are silver and gold,
   they are the work of human hands.

5 They have mouths, but do not speak;
   they have eyes, but do not see.
6 They have ears, but do not hear;
   they have noses, but do not smell.

7 They have hands, but do not feel;
   they have feet, but do not walk;
   they utter no sound from their throats.
8 Their makers will end up like them,
   so are all who trust in them.

9 O Israel, trust in Yahweh!
   your Helper and your Shield.
10 O house of Aaron, trust in Yahweh!
   your Helper and your Shield.

11 You Who revere Yahweh, trust in Yahweh!
   your Helper and your Shield.
12 Yahweh remembers us and will bless us;
   will bless the house of Israel;
   will bless the house of Aaron;

13 will bless those who revere Yahweh,
   both the small and the great.
14 May Yahweh add to your numbers,
   to yours and to your children's!

15 May you be blessed by Yahweh,
   Who made heaven and earth!
16 The heavens belong to Yahweh,
   but the earth, Yahweh gave to humanity.

17 The dead do not praise Yahweh,
   nor do any who sink into silence.
18 But we will bless Yahweh
   henceforth and forevermore.
   Praise Yahweh!

PSALM 116
Hymn of Thanksgiving for Deliverance
from Death

1   I love Yahweh
     Who listens to the sound of my prayer,
2   Who bends down to listen to me,
     Whom I will implore all my life.

3   The traps of death encircled me;
     the agony of Sheol came upon me;
     I was overcome by distress and anguish.
4   Then I called on the Name of Yahweh:
     "Deliver me, Yahweh, I beseech You.

5   O Yahweh, You are gracious and just;
     O God, You are compassionate.
6   O Yahweh, You look after the simple;
     when I was powerless, You gave me strength."

7   "Return, O my soul, to your rest;
     for Yahweh has treated you kindly."
8   "For You have rescued my soul from death,
     my eyes from tears, my feet from stumbling;
9   that I may walk before You, Yahweh,
     in the land of the living."

10   I kept my faith, even when I said,
     "I am awfully distressed;"
11   In my fright, I said,
     "No human being can be relied on."

12   What return can I make,
     for all the good Yahweh has done me?
13   I will lift up the cup of salvation
     and call on the name of Yahweh,

14   I will fulfill my vows to Yahweh
     in the presence of all the people.

15   Precious in the sight of Yahweh
     is the death of the holy ones.

16   Truly I am Your servant now,
     O Yahweh, I am Your servant,
     for I am the child of Your slave;
     You have broken my fetters.
17   I will offer You a sacrifice of thanksgiving
     and call on Your Name, O Yahweh.

18   I will fulfill my vows to Yahweh
     in the presence of all the people,
19   in the courts of the house of Yahweh,
     in your midst, O Jerusalem.
     Praise Yahweh!

PSALM 117
An Invitation to All Nations to Praise Yahweh

1   Praise Yahweh, all you nations!
    Acclaim Yahweh, all you peoples!

2   For Yahweh's faithful love is mighty,
    and Yahweh's faithfulness everlasting.

    Praise Yahweh!

PSALM 118
Royal Hymn of Thanksgiving for Victory

1   O give thanks to Yahweh, Who is good,
    Whose faithful love endures for ever.

2   Let Israel say,
    "God's faithful love endures for ever."
3   Let the house of Aaron say,
    "God's faithful love endures for ever."
4   Let those who revere Yahweh say,
    "God's faithful love endures for ever."

5   In my distress I called to Yahweh;
      Yahweh answered me and set me free.

6   Yahweh is with me and I will not fear.
      What can human beings do to me?

7   Yahweh is with me, my Helper,
      I shall see my foes confounded.

8   It is better to take refuge in Yahweh
      than to rely on human beings.

9   It is better to take refuge in Yahweh
      than to rely on earthly rulers.

10   All the nations swarmed around me;
      in the name of Yahweh I cut them down!

11   They swarmed around me, pressing upon me;
      in the name of Yahweh I cut them down!

12   They swarmed around me like hornets,
      they blazed like a fire of thorns;
      in the name of Yahweh I cut them down!

13   I was pushed hard, so that I was falling,
      but Yahweh came to my help.

14   Yahweh is my strength and my song;
      and has become my saving justice.

15   Shouts of rejoicing and victory
      are in the tents of the just:
      "Yahweh's right hand is triumphant,

16   Yahweh's right hand is victorious,
      Yahweh's right hand is triumphant."

17   I shall not die, but I shall live,
      to recount the great deeds of Yahweh.

18   Yahweh has chastised me severely,
      but has not given me over to death.

19   Open for me the gates of saving justice,
      that I may go in to give thanks to Yahweh.

20   This is the gate of Yahweh;
      into which the just shall enter.

21 I thank You that You have answered me
   and have become my saving justice.

22 The stone which the builders rejected
   has become the headstone of the corner.

23 This is Yahweh's doing;
   it is marvelous in our eyes.

24 This is the day which Yahweh has made;
   let us rejoice and be glad in it.

25 Save us, we beseech You, O Yahweh!
   O Yahweh, we beseech You, give us success!

26 Blessed be the one who comes in the name of Yahweh!
   We bless You from the house of Yahweh.

27 O Yahweh, our God, enlighten us.

   Link your processions, branches in hand
   up to the horns of the altar!

28 You are my God, I thank You;
   you are my God, I praise You.

29 O give thanks to Yahweh, Who is good;
   Whose faithful love endures for ever!

PSALM 119
Meditative Psalm in Praise of God's Law

ALEPH

1 Blessed are those whose way is perfect,
  who walk in the law of Yahweh!

2 Blessed are those who keep Your instructions,
  who seek You with their whole heart,

3 who also do no wrong,
  but walk in Your ways!

4 It was You Who commanded
  Your precepts to be diligently observed.

5 O that my ways were faithful
   in observing Your statutes!
6 Then I should not be ashamed,
   when I look to all Your commands.

7 I will praise You with integrity of heart,
   as I learn Your just decrees.
8 I will observe Your statutes;
   do not forsake me, O eternal One!

BETH

9 How can the young keep their way pure?
   By guarding it according to Your word.
10 I have sought You with my whole heart;
   let me not wander from Your commands!

11 I have enclosed Your promise in my heart,
   that I might not sin against You.
12 Blessed are You, O Yahweh;
   teach me Your statutes!

13 With my lips I have proclaimed
   all the decrees of Your mouth.
14 I have rejoiced in the way of Your instructions
   more than in all riches.

15 I have meditated on Your precepts,
   and am familiar with Your ways.
16 I will delight in Your statutes;
   I will not forget Your words.

GIMEL

17 Deal bountifully with Your servant,
   that I may live and observe Your word.
18 Open my eyes, that I may behold
   wondrous things out of Your law.

19 I am a sojourner on earth;
    hide not Your commands from me!
20 My soul is consumed with longing
    for Your decrees in every season.

21 You have rebuked the arrogant, the accursed,
    who go astray from Your commands.
22 Remove from me reproach and contempt,
    for I have kept Your instructions.

23 The ungodly sat and plotted against me,
    but Your servant will meditate on Your statutes.
24 Your instructions are my delight,
    Your wishes my counselors.

DALETH

25 I lie prostrate in the dust;
    revive me according to Your word!
26 I have recounted my ways and You heard me;
    teach me Your statutes!

27 Make me understand the way of Your precepts,
    and I will meditate on Your wondrous works.
28 My soul melts away with grief;
    raise me according to Your word!

29 Remove from me the way of lying;
    and graciously teach me Your law!
30 I have chosen the way of truth,
    I set Your decrees before me.

31 I have clung to Your instructions,
    O Yahweh, do not put me to shame!
32 I will run the way of Your commands
    if You enlarge my understanding!

HE

33 Teach me, O Yahweh, the way of Your statutes;
    and I will keep it to the end.

34 Give me understanding, that I may keep Your law
     and observe it with my whole heart.

35 Direct me in the path of Your commands,
     for my delight is therein.
36 Incline my heart to Your instructions,
     and not to unjust gain!

37 Turn my eyes from looking at vanities;
     and restore my life in Your ways.
38 Confirm Your promise to Your servant,
     who is faithful in revering You.

39 Remove the reproach because I revere You;
     for Your decrees are good.
40 See how I yearn for Your precepts;
     in Your saving justice give me life!

WAW

41 Let Your faithful love come to me, Yahweh,
     save me according to Your promise.
42 Give me an answer to those who provoke me,
     for I trust in Your word.

43 Remove not the word of truth out of my mouth,
     for my hope is in Your decrees.
44 I will keep Your law without fail,
     for ever and ever.

45 I shall live in all freedom,
     for I have sought Your precepts.
46 I shall speak of Your instructions before rulers,
     and will not be ashamed.

47 I find delight in Your commands,
     I love them dearly.
48 I revere Your commands, which I love,
     and I will meditate on Your statutes.

ZAYIN

49　Remember Your word to Your servant,
　　upon which You made me rest my hope.
50　This is my comfort in my affliction
　　that Your promises restored me to life.

51　The arrogant ridiculed me incessantly
　　but I have not strayed from Your law.
52　I have remembered Your decrees of old,
　　truly, O Yahweh, I am comforted.

53　Fury grips me when I see the wicked
　　who abandon Your law.
54　Your statutes have been my songs
　　in the house of my pilgrimage.

55　All night I have remembered Your Name,
　　and have observed Your law, O Yahweh.
56　This has been my practice,
　　and I have kept Your precepts.

HETH

57　You are my portion, O Yahweh,
　　I promise to observe Your word.
58　I entreat Your favor with all my heart;
　　be gracious to me according to Your promise.

59　I considered Your ways,
　　I turn my steps to Your instructions.
60　I hastened and did not delay
　　to observe Your commands.

61　Though the wicked encircled me,
　　I did not forget Your law.
62　At midnight I rise to praise You,
　　because of Your just decrees.

63 I am a companion of all who revere You,
    of all who observe Your precepts.
64 The earth is full of Your faithful love;
    O Yahweh, teach me Your statutes!

TETH

65 You have dealt well with Your servant,
    O Yahweh, according to Your word.
66 Teach me good judgment and knowledge,
    for I believe in Your commands.

67 Before I was humbled I used to go astray,
    but now I keep Your promise.
68 You are good and the cause of good;
    teach me Your statutes.

69 The arrogant besmear me with lies,
    but I observe Your precepts with all my heart.
70 Their heart is like fat without feeling
    but I delight in Your law.

71 It was good for me that I was humbled,
    that I might learn Your statutes.
72 More precious to me is the law from Your mouth,
    than thousands of gold and silver pieces.

YODH

73 Your hands have made me and fashioned me;
    give me insight that I may learn Your commands.
74 Those who revere You shall see me and rejoice,
    because I have hoped in Your word.

75 I know, Yahweh, that Your decrees are right,
    and that You, in faithfulness, have humbled me.
76 Let Your faithful love be my comfort
    according to Your promise to Your servant.

77 Treat me with tenderness and I shall live,
    for Your law is my delight.
78 Let the arrogant who lie against me be shamed,
    while I ponder Your precepts.

79 Let those who revere You turn to me,
    that they may know Your instructions.
80 May my heart be perfect in Your statutes,
    that I may not be ashamed.

KAPH

81 My soul yearns for Your salvation;
    I hope in Your word.
82 My eyes grow bleary awaiting Your promise;
    I ask, "When will You comfort me?"

83 For I have suffered all disgrace,
    yet I have not forgotten Your statutes.
84 How many are the days of Your servant?
    When will You bring my persecutors to judgment?

85 The arrogant have dug a pit for me,
    they are not in conformity with Your law.
86 All Your commands are trustworthy;
    help me when they oppress me dishonestly.

87 They nearly erased me from the earth;
    but I did not renounce Your precepts.
88 In Your faithful love spare my life,
    and I will keep the instructions of Your mouth.

LAMEDH

89 For ever You are, O Yahweh,
    Your word is firmly fixed in the heavens.
90 Your constancy endures to all generations;
    You established the earth, and it stands firm.

91　They continue to abide according to Your decrees,
　　for all things are Your servants.

92　Had not Your law been my delight,
　　I should have perished in my affliction.

93　I will never forget Your precepts;
　　for by them You have given me life.

94　I am Yours, save me;
　　for I have sought Your precepts.

95　The wicked lie in wait to destroy me;
　　but I ponder over Your instructions.

96　To all perfection I have seen a limit,
　　but Your Commandments have no limit.

MEM

97　Oh, how I love Your law!
　　I meditate on it all day long.

98　Your Command makes me wiser than my foes,
　　because it is ever with me.

99　I have more wisdom than all my teachers,
　　for Your instructions are my meditation.

100　I have more insight than the elders,
　　for I keep Your precepts.

101　I have kept my feet from every evil path,
　　in order to keep Your word.

102　I have not departed from Your decrees,
　　since You Yourself have taught me.

103　How pleasant is Your promise to my palate,
　　yes, sweeter than honey to my mouth!

104　From Your precepts I gain insight;
　　so I hate all deceptive ways.

NUN

105　Your word is a lamp for my feet
　　a light on my path.

106 I have sworn and will persevere
     in observing Your just decrees.

107 I am sorely afflicted, O Yahweh;
     give me life according to Your word!

108 Accept, Yahweh, my offerings of praise,
     and teach me Your decrees.

109 My life is in Your hands for ever,
     let me not forget Your law.

110 The wicked have laid a snare for me,
     but I have not strayed from Your precepts.

111 Your instructions are my eternal heritage,
     they are the joy of my heart.

112 I devote myself to obeying Your statutes,
     their recompense is eternal.

SEMEKH

113 I hate a divided heart,
     but I love Your law.

114 You are my Protector and my shield;
     I hope in Your word.

115 Depart from me, you wicked,
     that I may observe the commands of my God.

116 True to Your promise, sustain me and I shall live,
     do not let me be ashamed in my hope.

117 Uphold me and I shall be saved,
     that I may always respect Your statutes.

118 You reject all who go astray from Your statutes;
     for they worship falsehood.

119 You reject as dross all the wicked of the earth,
     so I love Your instructions.

120 My whole body trembles before You,
     Your decrees fill me with awe.

AYIN

121 I have practiced Your just decrees;
do not hand me over to my oppressors.
122 Assure the well-being of Your servant;
do not let the arrogant oppress me.

123 My eyes are languishing for Your salvation,
and for the promise of Your saving justice.
124 Deal with me according to Your faithful love,
and teach Your servant Your statutes.

125 Give me understanding, I am Your servant;
that I may know Your instructions.
126 It is time to take action, Yahweh,
for Your law is being broken.

127 So I love Your commands
more than gold, purest gold.
128 So I consider right all Your precepts,
I hate all ways of falsehood.

PE

129 Your instructions are wonderful;
so my soul observes them.
130 The unfolding of Your word gives light;
it imparts insight to the simple.

131 With gasping mouth I panted,
in my yearning for Your commands.
132 Turn to me and be gracious to me,
as is Your decree to those who love Your Name.

133 Steady my steps according to Your promise,
let not wickedness triumph over me.
134 Rescue me from human oppression,
that I may observe Your precepts.

135 Make Your face shine upon Your servant,
and teach me Your statutes.

136 My eyes shed streams of tears,
     because Your law is not observed.

TSADE

137 O Yahweh, You are just,
     Your decrees are fitting.
138 You have established Your instructions
     in justice and perfect faithfulness.

139 My zeal is burning me up,
     because my enemies ignore Your word.
140 Your promise is well tested
     and Your servant holds it dear.

141 I am insignificant and abject,
     yet I do not forget Your precepts.
142 Your justice is eternally just,
     and Your law is trustworthy.

143 Distress and anguish have come upon me,
     but Your commands are my delight.
144 Your instructions are eternally just,
     give me insight that I may live.

QOPH

145 I call with all my heart, Yahweh, answer me,
     and I will observe Your statutes.
146 I call to You; save me,
     and I will keep Your instructions.

147 I rise before dawn and call for help;
     I put my hope in Your word.
148 My eyes are awake before each watch of the night,
     that I may ponder Your promise.

149 In Your faithful love, Yahweh, listen to my voice,
     let Your decrees give me life.

150 The pursuers of corruption draw near;
    they are far from Your law.

151 But You are near, O Yahweh,
    and all Your commands are truth.

152 Long ago I learned from Your instructions
    for You have established them for ever.

RESH

153 Look on my affliction and deliver me,
    for I do not forget Your law.

154 Invoke my cause and reclaim me;
    give me life according to Your promise!

155 Salvation is far from the wicked,
    for they do not seek Your statutes.

156 Your kindnesses to me are countless, Yahweh,
    true to Your decrees, give me life.

157 Countless are my oppressors and adversaries,
    but I do not deviate from Your instructions.

158 The sight of these traitors grieves me,
    because they do not observe Your promise.

159 See how I love Your precepts, O Yahweh,
    Give me life true to Your faithful love.

160 The essence of Your word is truth;
    and all Your just decrees endure for ever.

SHIN

161 Rulers persecute me without cause,
    because my heart delights in Your word.

162 I rejoice at Your promise
    as one who finds great fortune.

163 I detest and disdain deceit,
    but I cherish Your law.

164 Seven times a day I praise You
     for Your just decrees.

165 Great peace is to those who love Your law;
     nothing can make them stumble.

166 I wait for Your salvation, O Yahweh,
     and I follow Your commands.

167 My soul observes Your instructions;
     and I love them very much.

168 I observe Your precepts and instructions,
     for all my ways are known to You.

TAU

169 May my cry come into Your presence, Yahweh;
     give me wisdom according to Your word!

170 May my prayer come into Your presence;
     rescue me according to Your promise!

171 May my lips proclaim Your praise
     for You have taught me Your statutes.

172 May my tongue recite Your promise,
     for all Your commands are just.

173 May Your hand be ready to help me,
     for I have chosen Your precepts.

174 I long for Your salvation, Yahweh,
     Your law is my delight.

175 May I live only to praise You,
     may Your decrees be my help.

176 If I should go astray like a lost sheep,
     come and look for Your servant,
     for I have not forgotten Your commands.

PSALM 120
Prayer for Relief from Bitter Enemies

A Song of Ascents.

1 In my distress I called to Yahweh,
   and Yahweh answered me.
2 "O Yahweh, save me from lying lips,
   and from a deceitful tongue."

3 What more shall be given to you?
   What more shall be added to you?
   O deceitful tongue,
4 Like sharpened arrows of a warrior
   like glowing coals of the broom tree.

5 Woe to me, that I sojourn near Meshech,
   that I dwell near the tents of Kedar!

6 Too long have I had my dwelling,
   among people who hate peace.
7 As for me, when I speak of peace;
   they are all for war.

PSALM 121
Hymn to Yahweh, the Guardian of Israel

A Song of Ascents.

1 I raise my eyes to the Mountain,
   whence will help come to me?
2 My help comes from Yahweh,
   Who made heaven and earth.

3 Yahweh will not let your foot to slip,
   Yahweh, your guardian will not slumber.
4 Behold, the guardian of Israel
   shall neither sleep nor slumber.

5 Yahweh is your guardian;
   Yahweh is your shade on your right hand.

6 The sun shall not scourge you by day,
   nor shall the moon by night.

7 Yahweh will guard you from all evil;
   Yahweh will guard your life.
8 Yahweh will guard your goings and comings
   henceforth unto eternity.

PSALM 122
Pilgrim's Blessings on the Holy City

A Song of Ascents. Of David.

1 I rejoiced when I heard them say,
   "Let us go to the house of Yahweh!"
2 At last we have set foot,
   within your gates, O Jerusalem!

3 Jerusalem, built as a city
   which is bound firmly together,
4 There the tribes go up,
   the tribes of Yahweh.

   It is a decree for Israel
   to give thanks to the Name of Yahweh.
5 In it are established thrones of justice,
   the thrones of the house of David.

6 "May they pray for your peace, Jerusalem!
   May they prosper who love you!
7 Let there be peace within your walls,
   and prosperity within your dwellings!"

8 For the sake of my relatives and companions,
   I will say, "Peace be within you!"
9 For the sake of the house of Yahweh our God,
   I will pray for your well-being.

PSALM 123
Collective Entreaty for God's Mercy

A Song of Ascents.

1 I raise my eyes to You,
   Who are enthroned in heaven!
2 Like the eyes of a servant
   are on the hand of his master,

   Like the eyes of a servant
   are on the hand of her mistress,
   so our eyes are on You, Yahweh our God
   till You are gracious to us.

3 Be gracious to us, O Yahweh, be gracious to us,
   for we have been sated with contempt.
4 Our souls are more than sated
   with the mockery of the arrogant,
   with the contempt of the haughty.

PSALM 124
Collective Hymn of Thanksgiving

A Song of Ascents. Of David.

1 If it had not been Yahweh Who was on our side,
   —let Israel repeat it—
2 if it had not been Yahweh Who was on our side,
   when mortal enemies rose up against us,
3 then they would have swallowed us alive,
   when their wrath blazed against us.

4 Then they like the flood would have swept us away,
   the deluge would have swept over us;
5 over us would have swept the raging waters.

6 Blessed be Yahweh for not letting us fall
   like prey to their teeth!
7 We escaped like a bird from the fowlers' net;
   the net was broken, and we escaped!

8 Our help is in the name of Yahweh,
   Who made heaven and earth.

PSALM 125
Prayer for Deliverance from
National Enemies

A Song of Ascents.

1 Those who trust in Yahweh are like Mount Zion,
   unshakeable, it remains there for ever.
2 As the mountains encircle Jerusalem,
   so Yahweh encircles the chosen people,
   henceforth and for ever.

3 The scepter of the wicked shall not rest
   over the land allotted to the just,
   provided the just do not extend
   their hands to do what is unjust.

4 Show Your goodness, O Yahweh, to the good,
   and to the just in their hearts!
5 But as for those who follow their crooked ways
   may Yahweh scatter them with the evildoers!

   Peace be upon Israel!

PSALM 126
Collective Prayer for Restoration of Zion

A Song of Ascents.

1 When Yahweh brought back the captives of Zion,
   we were like those who dream.

2 Then our mouth was filled with laughter,
   and our tongue with shouts of joy;
   then they said among the nations,
   "Yahweh has done great things for them."

3   Yahweh has done great things for us;
    we are glad indeed.
4   Restore our fortunes, O Yahweh,
    like the streams in the Negeb!

5   Those who sow in tears
    shall reap with joyful shouts!
6   Those that go forth weeping,
    bearing the seed for sowing,
    shall come home with shouts of joy,
    bringing their sheaves with them.

PSALM 127
Trust in God the Sustainer

A Song of Ascents. Of Solomon.

1   If Yahweh does not build the house,
    its builders labor in vain.
    If Yahweh does not guard the city,
    its guards keep watch in vain.

2   In vain you get up earlier,
    put off going to bed,
    and eat the bread of toils,
    since it is the Reliable Who provides
    for the chosen ones as they sleep.

3   Indeed, children are a legacy from Yahweh,
    the fruit of the womb a reward.
4   Like arrows in the hand of a warrior
    are the children of one's youth.

5   How blessed are those
    who have filled their quivers with them!
    They shall not be put to shame
    but shall drive back the foes from the gate.

PSALM 128
Rewards of Those Who Trust in God

A Song of Ascents.

1 Blessed are those who revere Yahweh,
   and those who walk in God's ways!

2 You shall eat the fruit of your handiwork;
   you shall be happy and prosperous.
3 Your spouse will be like a fruitful vine
   by the sides of your house;
   your children will be like olive plants
   around your table.

4 Behold, thus one is blessed,
   who reveres Yahweh.
5 May Yahweh bless you from Zion!
   May you see the prosperity of Jerusalem
   all the days of your life!
6 May you see your children's children!

   Peace be upon Israel!

PSALM 129
A Prayer for the Defeat of Israel's Enemies

A Song of Ascents.

1 "Many times have they oppressed me since my youth,"
   —let Israel repeat it—

2 "Many times have they oppressed me since my youth,
   but they have not prevailed against me.
3 Upon my back the plowers plowed;
   upon it they made their furrows long."

4 May Yahweh the Just break
   the yoke of the wicked.
5 May they retreat in humiliation
   all those who hate Zion!

6 May they be like the grass on the housetops,
  which withers before the plucker's eyes,
7 which has not filled the hand of a reaper
  and the bosom of the binder of sheaves.

8 May those who pass by not say,
  "The blessing of Yahweh be upon you!
  We bless you in the name of Yahweh!"

PSALM 130
Prayer for Pardon and Mercy
Sixth Penitential Psalm

A Song of Ascents.

1 Out of the depths I cry to You, Yahweh!
2 Adonai, hear my voice!
  Let Your ears be attentive
  to my plea for mercy!

3 If You kept a record of our sins,
  Adonai, who could survive?
4 But with You is forgiveness,
  that You may be revered.

5 I have waited for You, O Yahweh,
  my being has waited for Your word.
6 My whole being waits for Adonai
  more than sentinels for daybreak;
  more than sentinels for daybreak,

7 let Israel wait for Yahweh!
  For with Yahweh is faithful love,
  with Yahweh is abundant redemption.
8 Yahweh will redeem Israel
  from all its sins.

PSALM 131
Psalm of Humble Trust in God

A Song of Ascents. Of David.

1 O Yahweh, my heart is not arrogant,
nor are my eyes raised too high.
I have taken no part in great affairs,
nor in wonders beyond my grasp.

2 I have kept my whole being quiet and silent,
like an infant quieted at its mother's breast;
like an infant quieted is my whole being.

3 Let Israel hope in Yahweh
henceforth for all eternity.

PSALM 132
The Covenant between Yahweh and David

A Song of Ascents.

1 Yahweh, remember David,
all the hardships he endured;
2 remember the oath he swore to Yahweh
and the vow to the Mighty One of Jacob:

3 "I will not enter the canopy of my house
will not climb into the bed spread for me;
4 I will not give sleep to my eyes
or rest to my eyelids,
5 until I find a place for Yahweh,
a dwelling for the Mighty One of Jacob."

6 Listen, we heard of it in Ephrathah,
we learned of it in the fields of Jaar.
7 "Let us go to Yahweh's dwelling,
let us worship at Yahweh's footstool!"

8 "Go up to Your resting-place, Yahweh,
You and the ark of Your strength.

9   May Your priests be clothed with justice,
    Your devoted ones shout for joy.
10 For the sake of David Your servant
    turn not away the face of Your anointed."

11 Yahweh has sworn a sure oath to David
    and will not turn back from this word:
    "I promise that I will set
    an offspring of yours on your throne.

12 If your children keep my covenant
    and my instructions which I teach them,
    their descendants too, forevermore,
    shall sit upon your throne."

13 For Yahweh has chosen Zion,
    and has desired it for a habitation:
14 "This is my resting-place for ever,
    here I will dwell, for I have desired it.

15 I will abundantly bless its breadwinners;
    I will satisfy its poor with bread.
16 I will clothe its priests with justice,
    and the devoted ones will shout for joy.

17 I will make a horn to sprout for David;
    I have prepared a lamp for my anointed;
18 whose enemies I will clothe with shame,
    but upon whom the crown will shed its luster."

PSALM 133
True Communion of God's People

A Song of Ascents.

1   How very good, how delightful it is
    when kindred live together in unity!

2   It is like the precious oil on the head,
    running down upon the beard,

running down upon Aaron's beard,
onto the collar of his robes!

3 It is like the dew of Hermon,
falling on the mountains of Zion.
For there Yahweh bestows the blessing,
life for evermore!

PSALM 134
Come Bless Yahweh at Night

A Song of Ascents.

1 Come, bless Yahweh,
all you who serve Yahweh,
who stand in the house of Yahweh,
through the watches of the night.

2 Lift up your hands to the sanctuary,
and bless Yahweh!

3 May Yahweh bless you from Zion,
the Maker of the heavens and earth!

PSALM 135
Hymn of Praise to the God of Creation

1 Praise Yahweh.

Praise the name of Yahweh,
give praise, you who serve Yahweh,
2 you who stand in the house of Yahweh,
in the courts of the house of our God!

3 Praise Yahweh, for Yahweh is good;
sing to God's name, it is delightful!
4 For Yahweh has chosen Jacob for oneself,
Israel as private possession.

5   For I know that Yahweh is great,
    and that our God is above all gods.
6   Everything that Yahweh is pleased to do
    Yahweh does in the heavens and on earth,
    in the seas and all deep places.

7   Yahweh causes the clouds to rise
    at the end of the earth,
    makes lightning for the rain,
    and brings the wind out of the vault.

8   Yahweh struck the first-born of Egypt,
    both of human beings and of animals.
9   Yahweh sent signs and wonders in your midst,
    O Egypt, on Pharaoh and on all his servants.

10 Yahweh struck down many nations,
    slew mighty rulers,
11 Sihon, ruler of the Amorites,
    Og, ruler of Bashan,
    and all the rulers of Canaan,
12 and gave their land as a heritage,
    a heritage to the people of Israel.

13 Your Name, O Yahweh, endures for ever,
    Your renown, O Yahweh, to all generations.

14 For You, Yahweh, vindicate Your people,
    and have compassion on Your servants.
15 The idols of the nations are silver and gold,
    the work of human hands.

16 They have mouths, but speak not,
    they have eyes, but see not,
17 they have ears, but hear not,
    nor is there breath in their mouths.
18 Their makers will become like them!
    and every one who trusts in them!

19 O house of Israel, bless Yahweh!
O house of Aaron, bless Yahweh!
20 O house of Levi, bless Yahweh!
You who revere Yahweh, bless Yahweh!

21 Blessed be Yahweh from Zion,
the One Who dwells in Jerusalem!
Praise Yahweh!

PSALM 136
Hymn of Praise, "the Great Hallel"

1 O give thanks to Yahweh, Who is good,
Whose faithful love endures for ever.
2 O give thanks to the God of gods,
Whose faithful love endures for ever.
3 O give thanks to the Ruler of rulers,
Whose faithful love endures for ever;

4 Who alone does great wonders,
Whose faithful love endures for ever;
5 Who in wisdom made the heavens,
Whose faithful love endures for ever;
6 Who spread out the earth on the waters,
Whose faithful love endures for ever;

7 Who made the great lights,
Whose faithful love endures for ever;
8 the sun to rule over the day,
Whose faithful love endures for ever;
9 the moon and stars to rule the night,
Whose faithful love endures for ever;

10 Who struck the first-born of Egypt,
Whose faithful love endures for ever;
11 and brought Israel out from among them,
Whose faithful love endures for ever;

12 with a strong hand and an outstretched arm,
    Whose faithful love endures for ever;

13 Who divided the Red Sea into parts,
    Whose faithful love endures for ever;
14 and made Israel pass through the middle,
    Whose faithful love endures for ever;
15 but drowned Pharaoh and the army in the Red Sea,
    Whose faithful love endures for ever;

16 Who led Israel through the wilderness,
    Whose faithful love endures for ever;
17 Who struck down great rulers,
    Whose faithful love endures for ever;
18 and slaughtered famous rulers,
    Whose faithful love endures for ever;

19 Sihon, Ruler of the Amorites,
    Whose faithful love endures for ever;
20 and Og, Ruler of Bashan,
    Whose faithful love endures for ever;

21 and gave their land as a heritage,
    Whose faithful love endures for ever;
22 a heritage to Israel, the chosen one,
    Whose faithful love endures for ever.

23 Who remembered us when we were humbled,
    Whose faithful love endures for ever;
24 and rescued us from our enemies,
    Whose faithful love endures for ever;

25 Who gives food to all living creatures,
    Whose faithful love endures for ever.
26 O give thanks to the God of heaven,
    Whose faithful love endures for ever.

PSALM 137
Longing for Zion: Prayer of the Exiles

1   By the rivers of Babylon,
    we sat down and there we wept,
    when we remembered Zion.
2   On the willows in its midst
    we hung up our harps.

3   For there our captors asked us
    to sing to them songs,
    our plunderers, songs of gladness,
    "Sing us one of the songs of Zion!"

4   How could we sing a song of Yahweh
    in a foreign soil?
5   If I forget you, O Jerusalem,
    may my right hand wither!

6   May my tongue cleave to my palate,
    if I do not keep you in mind,
    if I do not count Jerusalem
    the greatest of my joys!

7   Remember, O Yahweh, the Edomites
    the day of Jerusalem's fall,
    for they said, "Raze it, raze it!
    Down to its foundations!"

8   Daughter of Babylon, doomed to destruction,
    Blessed are they who repay you
    the evil you have done us!
9   Blessed are they who seize your infants
    and dash them against the stones!

PSALM 138
Hymn of Thanksgiving for Yahweh's Goodness

A Psalm of David.

1 I give You thanks, O Yahweh, with all my heart;
    before the angels I sing Your praise;
2 I bow down before Your holy temple
    and give thanks to Your Name
    for Your faithful love and Your Truth;
    for You have exalted above all
    Your Name and Your promise.

3 On the day I called, You did answer me,
    my strength of soul You did increase.

4 All the rulers of the earth will praise You,
    when they hear the words of Your mouth;
5 and they will sing of Your ways,
    for great is the glory of Yahweh.
6 For though You, Yahweh, are exalted,
    You regard the lowly,
    though You are lofty,
    You heed even from a distance.

7 Though I walk surrounded by trouble,
    You preserve my life;
    You stretch out Your hand
    against the wrath of my enemies,
    Yahweh, Your right hand delivers me.
8 Your hand will do everything for me;
    Yahweh, Your faithful love endures for ever.
    Do not forsake the work of Your hands.

PSALM 139
Hymn to the Omniscient God

To the choir director. A Psalm of David.

1 O Yahweh, You observe me and know me!

2 You know when I sit and when I stand;
   You discern my thoughts from afar.
3 You watch when I walk or lie down,
   and are familiar with all my ways.

4 Even before a word is on my tongue,
   O Yahweh, You know all about it.
5 Behind and in front You fence me in,
   You lay Your hands upon me.
6 Such amazing knowledge is beyond me;
   it is too high, I cannot attain it.

7 Whither can I go to escape Your Spirit?
   Or whither can I flee from Your presence?
8 If I ascend into the heavens, You are there!
   If I descend into Sheol, You are there!

9 If I take the wings of the morning
   dwelling in the uttermost part of the sea,
10 even there Your hand shall guide me,
   and Your right hand shall hold me.

11 If I say, "Let the darkness cover me,
   and the night be light about me,"
12 even the darkness is not dark to You,
   the night is bright as the day;
   for darkness is as light with You.

13 For it was You Who formed my inmost parts,
   You knit me together in my mother's womb.
14 For so many marvels I praise You,
   for I am wonderfully made, O Most High.

   Marvelous are all Your works;
   and my soul knows it very well.
15 My being was not hidden from You,
   when I was being formed in secret,
   textured in the depths of the earth.

16 Your eyes beheld my life stages;
    in Your scroll were all of them inscribed
    the days that were formed for me,
    when as yet there was none of them.

17 How precious are Your thoughts for me,
    O God, how great have been their sum!
18 Were I to count them, they outnumber the sands.
    Were I to come to an end, I am still with You. ×

19 O that You, God, would destroy the wicked,
    and would keep the bloodthirsty away from me,
20 and those who maliciously speak against You,
    who lift themselves up against You for evil!

21 Do I not detest those who hate You, O Yahweh?
    do I not detest those who rise up against You?
22 With perfect hatred I detest them,
    they have become my enemies.

23 Search me, O God, and know my heart!
    Test me and know my thoughts!
24 See if there be any wicked way in me,
    and guide me on the way everlasting!

PSALM 140
Prayer for Deliverance from Violent Enemies

To the choir director. A Psalm of David.

1 Deliver me, O Yahweh, from the wicked;
   protect me from the violent,
2 who devise evil in their heart,
   and all day long conspire warfare.
3 They sharpen their tongues like a serpent,
   viper's venom is under their lips.

4 Guard me, Yahweh, from the hands of the wicked;
   protect me from the violent,
   who plan to trip up my steps.

5　The arrogant have hidden a trap for me,
　　with cords they have spread a net,
　　by the wayside they have set snares for me.

6　I say to Yahweh, You are my God;
　　listen, Yahweh, to the sound of my prayer.
7　Adonai, my God, my mighty Savior,
　　You are my helmet in the day of battle.
8　Grant not, O Yahweh, the desires of the wicked;
　　do not further their plan, lest they be exalted!

9　Do not let my attackers prevail,
　　let the evil of their own lips overwhelm them!
10　Let burning coals fall upon them!
　　Let them fall into deep pits, no more to rise!
11　Let not slanderers be established in the land;
　　let evil hunt down the violent into Exile!

12　I know that Yahweh defends the afflicted,
　　and executes justice for the needy.
13　Surely the just shall praise Your Name,
　　the honest shall dwell in Your presence.

PSALM 141
Prayer for Protection from Wickedness

A Psalm of David.

1　I call to You, Yahweh, hasten to me,
　　listen to my voice when I call to You!
2　May my prayer be set before You like incense,
　　my uplifted hands like an evening sacrifice!

3　Set, O Yahweh, a guard over my mouth,
　　guard, O Most High, the door of my lips!

4　Incline not my heart to an evil word,
　　to perform vicious deeds with the wicked;
　　in company with evildoers,
　　let me not partake of their delicacies!

5 Let the just chastise and rebuke me,
   it shall be a kindness;
   let not the wicked anoint my head with oil,
   for my prayer has been against their wickedness.

6 When their judges are stopped by a strong hand,
   let them hear Your words, for they are sweet.
7 Like the plowshare that scatters the earth,
   let their bones be scattered at the mouth of Sheol.

8 I have lifted up my eyes to You, O Yahweh God;
   I have trusted in You, leave not my soul naked!
9 Save me from the traps that are set for me,
   and from the snares of evildoers!

10 Let all the wicked fall into their own nets,
   while I pass on my way.

PSALM 142
Prayer for Relief from Persecutors

A Maskil—An Instruction of David, when he was in the cave.
A Prayer.

1 I cry to Yahweh with a loud voice,
   I pray to Yahweh with a loud voice.
2 I pour out my grievance in Your Presence,
   I recount my anguish in Your Presence.

3 When my spirit collapses within me,
   then You take notice of my way!
   In the way along which I walk
   they have hidden a trap for me.

4 I look to the right and see,
   there is no one who recognizes me.
   Every escape is hidden from me,
   there is no one who cares for me.

5 I cry out to You, O Yahweh;
   I profess, "You are my refuge,
   my share in the land of the living."

6 Give ear to my cry,
    for I am brought very low!
    Deliver me from those who pursue me;
    for they are too strong for me!

7 Bring me out of the prison,
    that I may praise Your Name!
    The just will surround me;
    for You deal mercifully with me.

PSALM 143
A Penitent's Humble Entreaty
Seventh Penitential Psalm

A Psalm of David.

1 Hear my prayer, O Yahweh;
    give ear to my pleading!
    In Your faithfulness answer me,
    in Your saving justice!
2 Do not bring Your servant into judgment,
    for no one living is just in Your sight.

3 For the enemy has pursued my soul,
    has crushed my life to the ground,
    has made me dwell in darkness
    like those long dead.
4 My spirit within me has collapsed
    my heart within me is terrified.

5 I remember the days of old,
    I meditate on all that You have done;
    I ponder on all that Your hands have done.
6 I stretch out my hands to You;
    my soul thirsts for You like a thirsty land.

7 Make haste to answer me, O Yahweh!
    My spirit languishes, O El!
    Hide not Your face from me,
    lest I be like those who sink into the Pit.

8 Cause me to hear of Your mercy at the dawn,
   for I place my trust in You.
   Cause me to know the way I should walk,
   for I lift up my soul to You.

9 Rescue me from my enemies, O Yahweh!
   To You I have fled for refuge!
10 Teach me to do Your will,
   for You are my God!
   Lead me into the land of justice,
   for Your Spirit is generous.

11 For the sake of Your Name, O Yahweh,
   preserve my life!
   In Your saving justice
   bring my soul out of distress!

12 And in Your faithful love
   disperse my enemies,
   and destroy all my adversaries,
   for I am Your servant.

PSALM 144
A Prayer of Thanksgiving for Prosperity

A Psalm of David.

1 Blessed be Yahweh, my Rock,
   Who trains my hands for war,
   and my fingers for battle;

2 my Faithful Love and my Fortress,
   my Stronghold and my Deliverer,
   my Shield and the One in Whom I take refuge,
   the One Who makes the peoples submit to me.

3 Yahweh, what is a human being for You to notice
   or who are humans that You think of them?
4 Our life is a mere puff of wind,
   our days are like a passing shadow.

5 Bow Your heavens, O Yahweh, and come down;
   touch the mountains and they shall smoke!
6 Flash Your lightning and scatter them,
   Forge Your arrows and conquer them!

7 Stretch down Your hand from on high,
   rescue me, save me from deep waters,
   from the hands of strangers,
8 whose mouths speak falsehood,
   whose right hand testifies to falsehood.

9 I will sing a new song to You, O God;
   I will play to You on a harp of ten strings.
10 It is You Who gives rulers their victories,
   Who rescues David, Your servant.

11 Rescue me from the cruel sword,
   and save me from the hands of strangers,
   whose mouths speak falsehood,
   whose right hand testifies to falsehood.

12 May our sons be like timber beams,
   vigorous from their youth;
   our daughters be like stone pillars
   hewn for the temple building.

13 May our store-houses be full,
   overflowing with produce of every kind,
   may our sheep increase by thousands,
   and tens of thousands in our fields;

14 may our cattle be heavy with young,
   may none among them be barren;
   may there be no raids and pillage,
   may our streets be free of mourning!

15 Happy are the people of whom this is true;
   Happy are the people whose God is Yahweh!

PSALM 145
Hymn Celebrating the Goodness of Yahweh
A Song of Praise. Of David.

1 I will glorify You, my God and Ruler,
and bless Your Name for ever and ever.

2 Day after day I will bless You,
and praise Your Name for ever and ever.

3 Yahweh, You are great and worthy of praise,
and Your greatness is inexpressible.

4 Each age will praise Your deeds to the next,
and shall proclaim Your mighty works.

5 O Majestic One, on Your glorious splendor,
and on Your wondrous works, I will ponder.

6 They will speak of Your awesome power,
and I shall recount Your great deeds.

7 They will proclaim the fame of Your goodness,
and shall joyfully acclaim Your saving justice.

8 Yahweh, You are gracious and merciful,
slow to anger and abounding in faithful love.

9 Yahweh, Your goodness extends to all,
and Your compassion to all Your creatures.

10 All Your creatures shall give thanks to You,
and Your devoted ones shall bless You!

11 They shall speak of the glory of Your dominion,
and tell of Your power.

12 They will make known to all Your mighty deeds,
and the glorious splendor of Your dominion.

13 Your reign is an everlasting reign,
and Your dominion lasts from age to age.

Yahweh, You are faithful in all Your words,
and gracious in all Your deeds.

14 Yahweh, You support all who stumble,
You raise up those who are bowed down.

15 The eyes of all look to You,
    and You give them their food in due season.
16 You open Your generous hands,
    and satisfy the desire of every living thing.

17 Yahweh, You are just in all Your ways,
    and faithful in all Your works.
18 Yahweh, You are near to all who call upon You,
    to all who call upon You in truth.

19 You fulfill the desire of all who revere You,
    You hear their cry, and save them.
20 You watch over all who love You;
    but all the wicked You will destroy.

21 My mouth will speak the praise of Yahweh,
    and all creatures will bless Your Holy Name,
    O Eternal and Everlasting!

PSALM 146
Hymn to Celebrate the Beneficence of Yahweh

1   Praise Yahweh!
    Praise Yahweh, O my soul!
2   I will praise Yahweh as long as I live;
    I will sing praises to my God all my life.

3   Do not put your trust in rulers,
    in human beings, who cannot save.
4   When their breath departs they return to the earth;
    on that very day all their plans come to nothing.

5   Happy are those whose help is the God of Israel,
    whose hope is in Yahweh, their God,
6   the Faithful One, Who made heaven and earth,
    the sea, and all that is in them.

7   Yahweh sets prisoners free,
    secures justice for the oppressed;
    gives food to the hungry.

8   Yahweh opens the eyes of the blind.
    Yahweh lifts up those who are bowed down;
    Yahweh loves the just.

9   Yahweh watches over sojourners,
    sustains the orphan and the widow,
    but blocks the way of the wicked.

10 Yahweh shall reign for ever,
    your God, O Zion, to all generations.
    Praise Yahweh!

PSALM 147
Hymn to Celebrate the Omnipotence of Yahweh

1   Praise Yahweh!
    it is good to sing praises to our God,
    it is fitting and delightful to sing praise.

2   Yahweh rebuilds Jerusalem,
    and gathers together the exiles of Israel.

3   Yahweh heals the brokenhearted,
    and binds up their wounds.

4   Yahweh sets the number of the stars,
    gives to all of them their names.

5   Our God is great and all-powerful;
    Whose understanding is beyond measure.

6   Yahweh sustains the destitute,
    but humbles the wicked to the ground.

7   Sing to Yahweh with thanksgiving;
    make melody to our God on the lyre!

8   Yahweh covers the heavens with clouds,
    provides the earth with rain,
    and makes grass grow upon the hills.

9   Yahweh gives animals their food,
    to the young ravens when they cry.

10 Yahweh takes no delight in the power of horses,
    no pleasure in the robustness of a warrior;

11 but takes pleasure in those who revere Yahweh,
     in those who hope in Yahweh's faithful love.

12 Praise Yahweh, O Jerusalem!
     Praise your God, O Zion!

13 For Yahweh strengthens the bars of your gates,
     and blesses your children within you.
14 Yahweh makes peace in your borders,
     and fills you with finest wheat.

15 Yahweh sends forth a word to the earth,
     the word that runs very swiftly.
16 Yahweh spreads snow like wool,
     and scatters hoarfrost like ashes.

17 Yahweh casts out hail like bread-crumbs,
     and who can withstand that cold?
18 Yahweh sends forth the word, and melts them;
     causes the wind to blow, and the waters flow.

19 Yahweh made promises to Jacob,
     and laws and ordinances for Israel.
20 Yahweh has not dealt thus with other nations;
     and has never taught them the precepts.
     Praise Yahweh!

PSALM 148
Cosmic Hymn of Praise of Yawheh, the Creator

1 Alleluia! Praise Yahweh!
    Praise Yahweh from the heavens,
    praise God from the heights!
2 Praise Yahweh, all you angels,
    praise God, all you legions!

3 Praise Yahweh, sun and moon,
    praise God, all you shining stars!
4 Praise Yahweh, you highest heavens,
    Praise God, you waters above the heavens!

213

5   Let them praise the Name of Yahweh!
    at Whose command they were made.
6   Yahweh established them for ever and ever,
    gave a decree that they not pass away.

7   Praise Yahweh from the earth,
    you sea monsters and all depths,
8   fire and hail, snow and frost,
    storm-winds that obey God's command!

9   Mountains and all hills,
    fruit trees and all cedars!
10 Wild animals and all cattle,
    reptiles and winged birds!

11 Rulers of the earth and all nations,
    princes and all judges on earth!
12 Young men and women together,
    older peoples and children too!

13 Let them praise the name of Yahweh,
    Whose name alone is exalted.
    The splendor of God's glory
    is above earth and heaven.

14 Yahweh heightens the strength of Israel,
    to the praise of all the faithful ones,
    the children of Israel, the people close to Yahweh.
    Praise Yahweh!

PSALM 149
Hymn to Celebrate the Justice of Yahweh

1   Praise Yahweh!
    Sing to Yahweh a new song,
    sing praise in the assembly of the faithful!
2   Let Israel rejoice in their Maker,
    let the children of Zion delight in their Ruler!
3   Let them praise the Name with dancing,
    let them sing praise to God with timbrel and lyre.

4 For Yahweh loves the chosen people;
and crowns the humble with victory.

5 Let the faithful exult in their Glorious One,
let them sing for joy on their couches.

6 Let the high praises of God be in their throats
and a two-edged sword in their hands,

7 to execute vengeance on the nations
and chastisement on the peoples,

8 to bind their rulers with chains
and their nobles with iron fetters,

9 to execute on them the verdict written,
and to give glory for all the saints.
Praise Yahweh!

PSALM 150
Hymn to the Creator: A Doxology

1 Alleluia! Praise Yahweh!

Praise Yahweh in the holy places;
praise God in the mighty firmament!

2 Praise Yahweh for mighty deeds;
praise God for sovereign majesty!

3 Praise Yahweh with trumpet sound;
praise God with harp and lyre!

4 Praise Yahweh with tambourines and dancing;
praise God with strings and pipes!

5 Praise Yahweh with clashing cymbals,
praise God with triumphant cymbals!

6 Let everything that breathes praise Yahweh!
Praise Yahweh! Alleluia!

ABOUT THE AUTHOR

Fr. Joseph J. Arackal, V.C., a member of the Vincentian Congregation, has a doctorate in ministry and has completed studies toward a doctorate in medieval history. He is conducting research on the biblical and theological foundations for the use of inclusive language and is working on a book entitled *A Theology of Inclusive Language*. He is the author of *Twenty-Two Gathering Prayers: Prayers in Inclusive Language for Church Council Meetings and Family and Community Gatherings* (Sheed & Ward, 1992), *Praying in Inclusive Language: Morning and Evening Prayer—The Four Week Psalter* (Patmos Publications, 1992), and *1993 International Worship and Freedom Appointment Calendar* (Patmos Publications, 1992).